Trauma-Informed Care

This accessible book provides an overview of trauma-informed care and related neuroscience research across populations. The book explains how trauma can alter brain structure, identifies the challenges and commonalities for each population and provides emergent treatment intervention options to assist those recovering from acute and chronic traumatic events. In addition, readers will find information on the risk factors and self-care suggestions related to compassion fatigue, and a simple rubric is provided as a method to recognize behaviors that may be trauma-related.

Topics covered include:

- children and trauma;
- adult survivors of trauma;
- military veterans and PTSD;
- sexual assault, domestic violence and human trafficking;
- compassion fatigue.

Trauma-Informed Care draws on the latest findings from the fields of neuroscience and mental health and will prove essential reading for researchers and practitioners. It will also interest clinical social workers and policy makers who work with people recovering from trauma.

Amanda Evans is Assistant Professor of Social Work at Florida Gulf Coast University in Fort Myers, USA. Her research relates to human trafficking, trauma and recovery, and she teaches courses in diagnosing psychopathology, direct practice, trauma and recovery, and loss and bereavement.

Patricia Coccoma is Associate Professor of Social Work at Florida Gulf Coast University, Fort Myers, USA. Her research focuses upon mental health, trauma and recovery, and she teaches graduate courses in direct practice.

Explorations in Mental Health series

Books in this series:

New Law and Ethics in Mental Health Advance Directives
The Convention on the Rights of Persons with Disabilities and the Right to Choose
Penelope Weller

The Clinician, the Brain, and I
Neuroscientific findings and the subjective self in clinical practice
Tony Schneider

A Psychological Perspective on Joy and Emotional Fulfillment
Chris M. Meadows

Brain Evolution, Language and Psychopathology in Schizophrenia
Edited by Paolo Brambilla and Andrea Marini

Quantitative and Qualitative Methods in Psychotherapy Research
Edited by Wolfgang Lutz and Sarah Knox

Trauma-Informed Care
How neuroscience influences practice
Amanda Evans and Patricia Coccoma

Trauma-Informed Care

How neuroscience influences practice

Amanda Evans and
Patricia Coccoma

Routledge
Taylor & Francis Group
LONDON AND NEW YORK

First published 2014
by Routledge
2 Park Square, Milton Park, Abingdon, Oxfordshire OX14 4RN

and by Routledge
711 Third Avenue, New York, NY 10017

First issued in paperback 2016

Routledge is an imprint of the Taylor & Francis Group, an informa business

British Library Cataloguing in Publication Data
A catalogue record for this book is available from the British
Library

Library of Congress Cataloging in Publication Data
Evans, Amanda, 1957- author.
Trauma-informed care : how neuroscience influences practice /
Amanda Evans and Patricia Coccoma.
pages cm
Includes bibliographical references (pages).
1. Psychic trauma--Patients--Rehabilitation. 2. Post-traumatic
stress disorder--Patients--Rehabilitation. 3. Crisis intervention
(Mental health services) 4. Traumatic neuroses--Patients--Services
for. I. Coccoma, Patricia, author. II. Title.
RC552.T7E83 2014
616.85'21--dc23
2013033533

ISBN 13: 978-1-138-63716-0 (pbk)
ISBN 13: 978-0-415-64012-1 (hbk)

Typeset in Bembo
by Saxon Graphics Ltd, Derby

Contents

Illustrations

Figure

Tables

Abbreviations

ACE	Adverse Childhood Experience Study
ACTH	adrenocorticotropic hormones
AL	allostatic load
APA	American Psychiatric Association
BPD	Borderline Personality Disorder
CAD	coronary artery disease
CATS	Child and Adolescent Trauma Treatment Services Project
CBT	Cognitive Behavioral Therapy
CCP	Child–Parent Psychotherapy
CCT	Cue-Centered Therapy
CDC	Centers for Disease Control and Prevention
CF	compassion fatigue
COPD	chronic obstructive pulmonary disease
CPT	Cognitive Processing Therapy
CRH	corticotrophin releasing hormones
CT	Cognitive Therapy
DBT	Dialectical Behavior Therapy
DESNOS	Disorders of Extreme Stress Not Otherwise Specified
DOD	Department of Defense
DSM	Diagnostic Statistical Manual
EI	Exposure Imagination
EMDR	Eye Movement Desensitization and Reprocessing
fMRI	functional magnetic resonance imaging
GAD	Generalized Anxiety Disorder
GCs	glucocorticoids
HAP	Humanitarian Assistance Program
HPA	hypothalamic-pituitary-adrenal
IPV	Interpersonal Partner Violence

IRT	International Relief Teams
MDD	Major Depressive Disorder
NATO	North Atlantic Treaty Organization
NCTIC	National Center for Trauma Informed Care
NCTSN	National Child Traumatic Stress Network
NET	Narrative Exposure Therapy
NMT	Neurosequential Model of Therapeutics
OEF	Operation Enduring Freedom
OIF	Operation Iraqi Freedom
PACT	Perceived Ability to Cope with Trauma scale
PCWRS	Parent–Child Weekly Rating Scale
PE	Prolonged Exposure
PET	Positive Emission Tomography
PFC	Prefrontal Cortex
PSS-SR	PTSD Symptom Scale Self Report
PTSD	Posttraumatic Stress Disorder
SAM	sympathetic-adrenal-medullary
SAMHSA	Substance Abuse and Mental Health Services Administration
SAS	sympathetic arousal system
SAS-CBT	Sexual Abuse Specific-Cognitive Behavioral Therapy
SC	Supportive Counseling
SCCT	Stanford Cue-Centered Therapy
SIPP	Statewide Inpatient Psychiatric Programs
SIT	Stress Inoculation Training
SITPE	Stress Inoculation Training with Prolonged Exposure
SNRIs	serum norepinephrine reuptake inhibitors
SOC	Sense of Coherence
SPARCS	Structured Psychotherapy for Adolescents Responding to Chronic Stress
SRILNAC	Sri Lankan National Counselors Association
SSRIs	serum serotonin reuptake inhibitors
STAIR	Skills Training in Affective and Interpersonal Regulation
STRIVE	Stress Resilience in Virtual Environments
STS	Secondary Traumatic Stress
TFC	Therapeutic Foster Care
TF-CBT	Trauma Focused-Cognitive Behavioral Therapy
TF-CTG	Trauma Focused-Childhood Grief
TFGT	Trauma Focused Group Therapy
TGC	Therapeutic Group Care
TREM	Trauma Recovery and Empowerment Model

TRM	Trauma Resiliency Model
UN	United Nations
VA	Veterans Affairs
VRET	Virtual Reality Exposure Therapy
WCDVS	Women Co-occurring Disorders and Violence Study
WHO	World Health Organization
WL	wait-listed

Acknowledgments

We would like to express our appreciation to Shannon Bradley, MSW, who served as a valuable contributor during the initial stages of locating research for this book. We would also like acknowledge the patience and support received from our families during all phases of this long process. We would finally like to thank our many colleagues who supported the concept of this text and provided valuable feedback related to direct practice application of trauma-informed care.

Chapter 1

Understanding trauma-informed care

Exposure to trauma may cause long-term distress in men, women, and children. There is little dispute among medical and mental health professionals that trauma and adversity can directly influence physical health and mental well-being. Across the globe, people experience catastrophes, interpersonal violence, war, and human rights violations. However, while social service and mental health professionals openly acknowledge this information, knowledge alone does not necessarily translate well into direct practice. In recent years, there has been global interest in concept of *trauma-informed* care. This term refers to an attempt to create a paradigm shift that encourages human service providers to approach their clients' personal, mental, and relational distress with an informed understanding of the impact trauma can have on the entire human experience. Advances in neuroscience research support a trauma-informed approach. While most people who experience traumatic events do not have residual symptoms to the point of qualifying as a disorder, many may experience clusters of symptoms that can interfere with social and occupational functioning. Creating systems with a focus on trauma-informed care calls for factoring "normal" responses to trauma into how providers conduct their daily business (NCTIC, n.d.; Ko, *et al.*, 2008; Harris and Fallot, 2001).

Emerging research on neurobiological changes that can occur within the human brain because of traumatic events has assisted in making the argument for implementing trauma-informed care. According to a wealth of neuroscience research, trauma can cause structural damage within the brain that contribute to adaptive behaviors in the brain's attempt to maintain safety (Liston, *et al.*, 2009; Juster, *et al.*, 2011). These adaptive processes, over time, become maladaptive and interfere with emotion regulation and attentional behaviors. These are the clients we see in practice. Trauma can contribute to depression (Thienkrua, *et al.*, 2006; Neria, 2010; Rao, *et al.*,

2010), anxiety (Derryberry and Reed, 2002; Goldin, *et al.*, 2009; Graham and Milad, 2011), and personality disturbances (Kobasa, 1979; Linehan, 1993; Haller and Miles, 2004).

In the United States, the National Center for Trauma-Informed Care articulates this paradigm shift as moving from asking, "What is wrong with you?" to one that asks, "What has happened to you?" (NCTIC, n.d.). In order to make this shift, we must:

1   move away from a pathology-based approach toward trauma survivors;
2   begin to recognize physical, relational, and emotional symptoms that may be a result of trauma exposure, but are often overlooked; and
3   implement services that incorporate best-practice methods for working with people who have survived traumatic events.

Understanding advances in neuroscience can assist care providers, mental health professionals, and medical practitioners to understand how trauma affects the human brain and influences behavior. Armed with this knowledge, there is the opportunity to examine past ways of understanding trauma and recovery and move toward new methods of assessment and intervention. New approaches and applications of neuroscience findings should attempt to create a bridge where gaps in recovery have been identified (Vieth, 2009) and should accommodate multicultural and multinational similarities and differences across societies worldwide (Miller, 2007).

The intent of this book is to assist practitioners in the application of knowledge gained from neuroscience related to trauma and to provide strategies and treatment techniques that have demonstrated efficacy for various populations. The authors intentionally designed the format not to be prescriptive regarding intervention methods. We attempted to identify interventions that have evidence of efficacy and appear to be congruent with neuroscience findings. A gap was identified in available research on interventions that may demonstrate portability across cultures. The few that were identified as demonstrating portable cultural application relied heavily on specialist practitioners for implementation (Errebo, *et al.*, 2008; Weiner, *et al.*, 2009). As we will discuss further, research on trauma and trauma interventions comes primarily from developed nations with mental health resources.

While the concept of trauma–informed care is gaining wide appeal in the United States, and other countries in the Western world, application of this approach varies from country to country and is not without its controversies. The reason for this has several dimensions:

1   many countries do not have the resources to assess and treat mental illness;

2   many countries and cultures hold negative stereotypes related to mental disorders; and

3   there is general mistrust regarding diagnostic labels and ascribing pathology to life events (World Health Organization, 2005; Rodin and van Ommeren, 2009).

Stigma and mental health

Globally, people who demonstrate symptoms of any mental dysfunction have experienced social stigma related to mental illness. In an attempt to mitigate this stigma, several countries have implemented national campaigns targeting the public's attitudes and stereotypes related to mental health with undetermined outcomes. While reliable outcome data on the impact of these campaigns is sparse, according to Vieth (2009) there is evidence that an education initiative introduced in Germany demonstrated some encouraging evidence of a diminished perception by the public that persons with schizophrenia were dangerous.

Stigma may be a contributing factor in the lack of data on mental health in many countries. In determining content for inclusion in this text, a comprehensive review of the literature was performed in order to identify strategies that may be useful not only in countries with extensive resources allocated to mental health, but also in lower-resource countries that may only have the ability to use specialists for the care of the most severely mentally ill. The cultural variances in trauma recovery and related research presented a challenge to the original intent of the authors, which was to create a text that combined knowledge obtained from neuroscience related to trauma across diverse populations and offer appropriate intervention methods obtained from the literature. The challenge of accomplishing this has been significant because the vast majority of the evidence-based literature on trauma recovery and mental health comes from Western countries, particularly the United States, which generally have specialized resources to treat mental disorders. However, research to meet this challenge revealed a larger global story; there is a lack of mental health research from most countries across the world.

Members of the Mental Health Research Mapping Project of the World Health Organization (WHO) and the Global Forum for Health Research conducted a comprehensive review of over 10,000 research articles related to international mental health. Their findings revealed that of the countries considered low–middle-income, 57 percent contributed fewer than five articles to the total mental health literature (Sharan, 2007). This dearth of research does not mean an absence of mental illness. In fact, epidemiology studies conducted by the WHO identified depression/anxiety, substance use disorders, and psychosis as the top three disorders worldwide, specifically as they affect children, adolescents, and women exposed to violence/trauma (Sharan, 2007). Lack of research resources dedicated to mental health may also reflect negative stigma related to mental health found in various resource-poor countries as it related to policy.

In the international arena, there has been considerable debate on the tendency to over-pathologize posttrauma human response (World Health Organization, 2005; Rodin and van Ommeren, 2009). Fear that an over-emphasis on trauma may lead to an increased practice of "labeling" people with mental illness has generated some well-deserved debate (Steel, 2009; Rodin and van Ommeren, 2009). The negative stigma related to mental health is prevalent in most countries, but in some to the extent that survivors fear being ostracized from their societies if they seek mental health treatment. Within the context of human rights, literature related to mental health and human rights violations has become more prolific since the establishment of diagnostic criteria for PTSD. While the concern regarding cultural applications of this criterion is valid, many researchers argue that the ability to use these criterion can play an important role in raising awareness regarding the extent and the impact of human rights violations (Steel, 2009).

Negative stigma related to mental illness also translates into policy. Findings from research prepared by the World Health Organization reveal that 37 percent of the countries in the world do not have a mental health policy. Low-and-middle-income countries (LMICs) spend less than 1 percent of their health budgets, which are limited, on mental health (World Health Organization, 2001). The lack of policy focus and funding for mental health results in research findings that are skewed toward interventions embraced by resource-rich countries. Therefore, most evidence-based interventions will largely be validated in countries with the resources to utilize mental health specialist to implement them. Given the global nature of trauma, reliance on mental health specialists alone to assist in trauma recovery is intrinsically flawed. However, the absence of research and methods that offer alternatives to this specialized approach to recovery creates challenges for change.

The call for a trauma-informed approach arises largely from an emerging acceptance that we, as providers of care, may be missing some fundamental issues that hinder a client's ability to integrate the trauma experience into their life and return to a reasonable sense of "normal." Many of these issues relate to safety. Additionally, after trauma, people try to cope. Sometimes, their methods of coping become destructive, such as abusing substances. According to Harris (2001), agencies that provide services for the homeless have long been aware of that many of their clients have significant trauma histories. However, these services are not focused on trauma, so past trauma is rarely addressed. A study by Christensen, *et al.* (2005) examined data collected from homeless individuals with co-occurring disorders over a one-year period. Their findings indicated that 79.5 percent of the clients evaluated had a history of physical or sexual abuse at some point in their lifetime. Within that same sample, all of the homeless women had a trauma history. At face value, it appears absurd to ignore a major life event that nearly 80 percent of a total population served experienced. However, many providers offer services that do not appear to relate to trauma, or perhaps even mental health. While they may know that their clients share this history, they are at a loss as to how to change their approach to services (Harris and Fallot, 2001). Even within the field of mental health, many providers have no training on trauma. Future innovative treatment strategies must assimilate what we know about biochemistry, social contexts, and environmental factors in order for mental health practitioners to move into the twenty-first century and successfully help trauma survivors (Miller, 2007).

The tendency to ascribe pathology to posttrauma responses is well documented and predominantly a Western society phenomenon (Micale, 2001). The Diagnostic and Statistical Manual (DSM), published by the American Psychiatric Association (APA) is widely used, even outside of the United States, as a method of standardizing clusters of symptoms that are severe enough to cause interference with social and occupational functioning (American Psychiatric Association, 2000). The term posttraumatic stress disorder (PTSD) was first recognized in the DSM in 1980 and was largely a result of advocacy work done on behalf of Vietnam veterans who were experiencing significant post-war mental distress and not receiving services (Micale, 2001). Since that time, the concept of PTSD has expanded beyond combat veterans and is often applied, perhaps overly, across populations.

However, trauma impacts survivors in more ways than the cluster of symptoms found in PTSD. There is some global concern related to the perception that there is a growing propensity to over-label persons with PTSD. Even within countries, such as the United States, that generally accepts the concept of PTSD, there is concern that the criteria are too narrow and ignore a variety of other issues that are also directly related to traumatic experiences (van der Kolk, 2002; Herman, 1992). Early childhood trauma can adversely impact the ability to develop relational trust that can be lifelong. Substance abuse, depression, anxiety disorders, and somatic illness can also be attributed to traumatic events (van der Kolk, 2002; van der Kolk, et al., 2005). These symptoms cluster under the title of Complex Trauma or Disorders of Extreme Stress Not Otherwise Specified (DESNOS). Herman (1992) has been a proponent for a broader understanding of survivors of chronic trauma for over three decades. In a comprehensive review of 50 years of research, Herman observed that survivors of prolonged trauma report symptoms that require an expanded perspective that goes beyond the diagnostic criteria of PTSD. According to Herman's research, survivors of prolonged trauma have higher rates of dissociation, anxiety disorders, suicidality, somatic complaints, and personality changes. Further research on the cumulative nature of prolonged exposure to trauma reveals that both adults and children demonstrate more complex symptoms of trauma (Cloitre, et al., 2009). These symptoms are evidenced in addition to the classic symptoms of PTSD, which include: hypervigilance, avoidance behaviors, recurrent and intrusive thoughts or images about the event, recurrent distressing dreams about the event, intense distress when exposed to internal or external cues that symbolize the event (American Psychiatric Association, 2000). While recognizing the severity of disruption symptoms of PTSD inflict on trauma survivors' lives, these criteria may be too narrow to understand the full implications of the impact of traumatic event (van der Kolk, et al., 2005). Improved understanding of how the brain responds to trauma enhances our ability to recognize the function of both adaptive and maladaptive behaviors, thoughts, and feelings. When the utility of these behaviors, thoughts, and feelings are understood and normalized by the survivor and practitioner, realistic tasks, interventions, and goals can be established. What makes trauma-informed care appealing is that it moves from an individual pathology perspective to a more holistic assessment of the impact of a trauma on all aspects of a trauma survivor's life (Capezza and Najavits, 2012). An in-depth discussion of this complexity is provided in Chapter 4 of this text.

Trauma-related illness

Over the past two decades, much has been written about the trauma and other co-occurring psychological symptoms. While the relationship of trauma to issues such as homelessness, mental illness, and substance abuse is well recognized, providers of services often treat them as distinct and separate issues. In the United States, the governmental agency, Substance Abuse and Mental Health Services Administration (SAMHSA) established a National Center for Trauma-Informed Care (NCTIC). According to their website, the NCTIC seeks to promote the adoption of trauma-informed care in a variety of settings including mental health, housing, domestic violence shelters, peer support groups, and victim assistance programs. The NCTIC encourage programs to recognize the following:

- a trauma survivor's need for respect, to be informed and hopeful during their recovery;
- the connection between trauma and symptoms of trauma (e.g., depression, anxiety, and substance-related disorders); and
- the need to work directly with survivors and their friends and family, and other provider organizations in a way that will lead to empowerment of survivors (NCTIC, n.d.).

The physical impact of stress is as detrimental to well-being as the emotional symptoms of stress. A review of the research done on stress over the past two decades reveals the need to approach the concept of stress-related illnesses from a broader interdisciplinary framework (Juster, *et al.*, 2011). Chronic stress, or threat, that activates the fear circuitry within the brain can disturb the immune system's ability to fight illness because of the overload of stress function. In a study by Bryant, *et al.* (2011), symptoms of 602 patients who had experienced a physically traumatic event were examined over a two-year period. Multiple heart rate recordings were taken beginning with the first contact with the patient and then again over time. The findings indicated that elevated heart rate in the acute phase following a traumatic event was also associated with the diagnoses of new cases of panic disorder, agoraphobia, and social phobia. The heart rate association was not found to correlate with Major Depressive Disorder (MDD) or Generalized Anxiety Disorder (GAD). These findings support earlier research that demonstrates a connection between fear-circuitry disorders and heart rate following trauma.

Chapters 4–8 in this text offer methods of intervention for trauma recovery that have demonstrated efficacy, been supported by research, and are considered "evidence-based." However, the risk of committing intellectual imperialism exists when any attempt is made to generalize specific treatment modalities across cultures. With this caution in mind, we encourage future research that examines how people recover from trauma *without* mental health specialists. Those insights may prove invaluable in understanding this complex issue.

Wars, famine, political violence, school-based violence, and cultural/religious conflict affect people across the globe. There is a need for cost-effective intervention strategies to help the citizens of the world recover from their experiences. The treatments methods described later in this book are not cost effective. Most are dependent upon postgraduate-trained specialists. In order for trauma care to move beyond the boundaries of industrialized nations, new methods must be identified.

Chapter 2

Understanding types of trauma

Advances in neuroscience over the years have validated the impact of social stressors on physical and emotional well-being by providing data related to the fear-circuitry system in the human brain (Sapolsky, *et al.*, 2000; Rodrigues, *et al.*, 2009). It is important to understand that the brain registers threat in a variety of ways. This response is a primal survival response and has contributed to keeping our species alive for millennia. However, in modern man and woman, the same stress response that galvanized us to flee from a charging mastodon − or to turn and attack it − is being utilized whenever we experience everyday social stress in general. Whether threat is real or perceptual, the brain responds by flooding the system with neurochemicals. When we neither flee nor fight, this flood of chemicals becomes toxic. This neurobiological response is discussed in depth in Chapter 3, but is important to keep in mind as we introduce a discussion of various types of trauma in this chapter.

The rationale for differentiating different types of trauma is a result of a review of the literature which demonstrates that there are some differences in how people experience, and recover, that may be relative to the type of trauma they experience. These include: personal trauma; trauma as a result of political situations; trauma in refugee populations; recovery from terrorist attacks; and environmental trauma such as natural disasters. The content in this chapter prepares the reader for more in-depth discussions related to various populations and their recovery challenges provided in Chapters 5, 6, 7, and 8. Within the subsequent chapters, we present similarities and differences related to population-specific types of trauma. The goal of presenting research findings in this manner is to assist practitioners to better understand the uniqueness of each survivor's experience while providing efficacious treatment methods for that population.

Personal trauma

There are many types of personal trauma such as rape, assault, accidents and injuries, human trafficking, and domestic violence. The presence of trauma alone is not necessarily an indicator that a person will experience long-term distress related to their experience (Sadock and Sadock, 2007). Statistically, most people who experience a traumatic event do not develop adverse symptoms significant enough to interfere with their social or occupational functioning (Harvey, 1996; Sadock and Sadock, 2007). The uniqueness of the individual's response to a traumatic event offers both hope and challenges for providers of trauma treatment. There is not a "one size fits all" approach to trauma recovery. Each practitioner is charged with conducting a comprehensive assessment of the client's strengths, needs, and abilities to help determine what treatment strategy may best suit their recovery requirements.

While every client is unique to their experience, there may be incident-specific or interpersonal variables that may contribute to, or buffer a client from, developing adverse symptoms related to personal trauma (Gutner, *et al.*, 2006; Irish, *et al.*, 2008). For instance, in the case of rape, one barrier to victim recovery may be linked to the relationship the client had with the perpetrator. Gutner, *et al.* (2006) examined coping strategies of rape survivors and the severity of posttrauma symptoms experienced by victims of sexual and physical assault. The findings indicated that the assault type, physical or sexual, was not a significant predictor of symptom severity. However, the relationship with the perpetrator appeared to be a stronger predictor of the likelihood of the survivor to develop severe symptoms. Survivors who were assaulted by strangers had higher rates of symptom severity and difficulty coping than those who knew their perpetrator. However, women who were raped by someone they knew were less likely to talk about the rape than someone who was assaulted by a stranger (Gutner, *et al.*, 2006). Self-blame is common in rape survivors and detrimental to recovery (Branscombe, *et al.*, 2003; Gunter, *et al.*, 2006; Littleton, *et al.*, 2009).

While all adverse life situations activate the same primal fear circuitry within the brain, a human brain has additional complexity of thoughts and feelings related to events. Therefore, the meaning of the traumatic experience varies from person to person. Personal trauma, such as rape, appears to have a more long-lasting negative affect than other types of trauma. An Australian study by Shakespeare-Finch and Armstrong (2010) measured posttrauma outcomes between survivors of motor vehicle accidents, sexual assault, and bereavement. This study was looking for positive outcomes that may have occurred as a result of the posttrauma process. The term used for positive posttrauma outcomes is called *posttraumatic growth*. Posttraumatic growth identifies positive changes that are interpreted by the survivor as a result of the struggle a person went through following a traumatic event (Tedeschi and Calhoun, 2004). The study by Shakespeare-Finch and Armstrong (2010) divided 94 trauma survivors into three groups: motor vehicle accidents, bereavement, and sexual abuse. Each group completed the Impact of Events Scale-Revised (Weiss and Marmar, 1997), which identifies symptoms of PTSD, and the Posttraumatic Growth Inventory (Tedeschi and Calhoun, 2004). The subjects in the bereavement groups reported significantly higher levels of growth in the domain related to appreciation of life when compared to the sexual abuse group. The same was true between those groups when examining posttraumatic growth in the domain of relating to others. All three groups were similar within the personal strength domain and the spiritual change domain. The subjects in the sexual assault group overwhelmingly scored higher levels of PTSD than those in the other two groups (Shakespeare-Finch and Armstrong, 2010). These findings reinforce the need for practitioners to assess not only traumatic experiences, but to be aware of how types of trauma may contribute to residual distress specific that that client.

Personal trauma has a confounding element that is different from the types of trauma experienced by war or natural disasters; personal trauma is often experienced in isolation from others. This isolation can contribute to feelings of shame, depression, and anxiety. As we will discuss in Chapters 4, 7, and 8, the isolation component of this trauma can be a barrier to recovery because it undermines intrinsic social support that the client might normally be able to openly access. Support from others can contribute significantly to recovery, regardless of culture, age, ethnicity, or type of trauma.

Political violence and trauma

Throughout recorded history, humans have waged war upon each other. Accounts of these events record winners and losers from a power perspective. However, the aftermath of political strife is far-reaching and goes beyond what is recorded in history books. In the wake of political violence, civilians suffer trauma-related after-effects long after treaties have been signed. There have been numerous studies assessing the long-term consequences of political violence on civilians. Survivors of the Nazi holocaust (Prot, 2010), African wars (Bokore, 2009), witnesses to the No Gun Ri killings in Korea

(Choi, S., 2011), children exposed to war in Lebanon (ElZein and Ammar, 2010), and Israeli civilians (Neria, 2010) all relate long-lasting residual symptoms from their trauma experiences.

Politicians and military spokespersons, to appease the conscience of the public, have used euphemistic terms such as "collateral damage," but it is difficult to hide behind a term when hundreds of thousands of the frail elderly, women, and children have suffered the devastating and long-lasting consequences of war. Under the cowardly context of war, women and girls are victims of repeated rape and degradation by soldiers and occupying soldiers. In many cultures, those same victims are abandoned by their families and ostracized by their society (Gingerich and Leaning, 2004).

Children are especially vulnerable to war and political violence. The life of a child usually involves school and play. However, children exposed to war violence often have trouble concentrating in school and engaging in play (ElZein and Ammar, 2010). They may experience depression, anxiety, and anger (Pine, *et al.*, 2005). Relationships can be disrupted which can lead to long-term attachment difficulties (Stauffer, 2009). An effect mechanism of war in many countries involves crimes of coercion and threat against children. One of the most chilling examples of atrocity is the forced labor of so-called "child soldiers." According to a comprehensive United Nations study on violence against children worldwide (Pinheiro, 2006), child soldiers range between the ages of 7–18. They are forced to participate in violence, act as cooks, sex slaves, or porters. In Uganda alone, over 25,000 children have been forced into being child soldiers over the past two decades. Klasen, *et al.* (2010) researched the effect of violence in a sample of 330 former child soldiers. All of the children had been abducted from their homes, and the mean age at the time of abduction was 10.8 years. More than half of the children in the sample had killed someone and one-fourth of them had been raped. The studied revealed that one-third of the children suffered from symptoms of PTSD, and more than one-third exhibited diagnostic symptoms of Major Depressive Disorder. Two-thirds exhibited behavioral and emotional problems that included anxiety, depression, physical complaints, and social problems.

While there is little doubt that political violence wreaks emotional havoc on the civilian population, as noted above, there are some encouraging studies that indicate that social support help mitigate the severity of the impact of violence (Neria, 2010; Radan, 2007). The impact of these findings is discussed in detail in Chapters 4 and 8 as they provide insight into the range of factors that contribute to trauma recovery.

Refugees and trauma

In 2010, it was estimated by the United Nations (UN) that there are 10.55 million refugees seeking asylum in a culture different from their own (UNHCR, 2011). Natural disasters, war, and political unrest contribute to this global phenomenon with more than half of the refugees being women and children. As a result of the US-initiated war in Afghanistan, Afghanis make up nearly one-third (three million) of the refugee population, most of whom have fled to Pakistan. Iraqi and Afghan refugees make up nearly half of all refugees worldwide. According to research findings, refugees suffer high rates of depression, anxiety disorders (including PTSD), substance abuse, and physical ailments. Many suffer feelings of loss and longing for their home. These feelings cause more distress than the impact of the trauma itself (Kirmayer, et al., 2011). In addition to the psychological distress noted above, children may also experience disorganized attachment to their caregivers as a result of having to flee their homes which can contribute to lifelong difficulties in forming and sustaining relationships (Stauffer, 2009).

Refugee status has been linked to mood disorders. Jamil and Ventimiglia (2010) examined the distribution of mental health disorders and length of treatment between refugees and non-refugees. The records of 191 Iraqi refugees were compared to 94 Arab, non-Iraqi, non-refugees, all of whom received services in Dearborn, Michigan. Dearborn contains the largest population of persons of Arab ethnicity in the United States. The findings of this research revealed higher rates of depression in Iraqi refugees compared to the non-refugees.

Refugees may also experience higher rates of other types of anxiety disorders that manifest in symptoms beyond PTSD. In a study of 126 adult Bosnian refugees, Silove, et al. (2010) found that adult separation anxiety was associated with PTSD but not with complicated grief or depression. In addition to the acute symptoms of PTSD, these adults experienced intense anxiety about being separated from loved ones and demonstrated exaggerated fear about harm happening to their close attachment figures.

The cultural loss experienced by refugees appears to exacerbate symptoms of trauma and may interfere with recovery. Research conducted by Bokore (2009) related to female survivors of wars in Somalia found that strong cultural traditions have been disrupted. While largely a tribal patriarchal society, Somali women develop a strong social support network with each other. However, the need to escape the war-torn regions in Somalia has forced many families to divide and immigrate to other countries, bringing with them memories of the atrocities they have left behind. As with any refugee group, they leave what is familiar and must adapt to new cultures and norms.

Because rape is a common method of degrading an enemy in Somalia, many women and young girls also struggle to cope with the impact of sexual assault. Culturally, this is additionally challenging because any discussion of sexuality, or reproductive health, is considered shameful. Therefore, these women and girls exist in a shroud of shame and suffer in silence.

Terrorism

A discussion of terrorism is especially applicable from a trauma-informed perspective because the goal of terror is to evoke fear. The fear circuitry of the brain is the primary system affected by trauma and involved in barriers to trauma recovery. Terrorist attacks often target civilian populations and are carried out by small groups within a society (Pine, et al., 2005). In Chapter 3 we discuss, in depth, the fear response within the brain, which will helps us better understand, from a neurobiological perspective, how destructive acts of terrorism can be. Unpredictable environments exacerbate the fear response within the brain because, as a survival mechanism, the brain is constantly trying to develop patterns that feel safe and secure.

Research on terrorism, and post-attack responses, is often focused on a particular event. The 9/11 attacks in the United States was the most deadly terrorist attack on US soil. Even those who were not in any of attack locations (New York, Washington, DC, and Pennsylvania) felt stress from the attacks nationwide. A study by Shuster, et al. (2001) conducted three to five days after the attacks utilized random-digit dialing to telephone numbers across the nation that resulted in a representative sample of 560 adults. Their findings revealed that 44 percent of adults surveyed reported one or more symptoms of stress related to the attacks. The level of stress experienced was associated with the extent of time the participants spent watching television coverage of the attacks. They identified religion, social support, and making donations as methods of coping.

Those directly affected by the attacks experienced more severe symptoms. Findings from a study conducted by Galea, et al. (2002) revealed that depression and PTSD were two times higher than baseline measurements five to eight weeks after the attacks on September 11, 2001. A study of 3,271 civilians who were evacuated from the World Trade Center Towers revealed that only 4.4 percent had no PTSD symptoms (DiGrande, et al., 2010). This study was conducted two to three years after the attack and the two most commonly identified symptoms were hyperarousal, and hypervigilance. According to Somer, et al. (2007), repeated threats of terrorism are probable predictors to psychological distress. This study explored civilian demoralization, coping (safety planning) strategies, and posttraumatic distress in relation to exposure to repeated terrorist threat in Israel. The findings of this research indicated that exposure to repeated acts of terror was correlated with posttraumatic distress. Low morale (demoralization) was significantly related to posttraumatic distress, emotion-regulating coping, solution-focused coping, and acceptance (Somer, *et al.*, 2007).

Pine, *et al.* (2005) identify some of the variances related to how children respond to acts of terrorism which are identified in the following principles:

1   the nature of the threat;
2   the stage of development of the children;
3   quality of family, peer, and school support – before and after the trauma; and
4   individual vulnerabilities and capabilities.

These principles are evident in the literature related to the neuroscience data on the developing brain of a child and the impact of trauma and effective treatment methods for treating traumatized children. An in-depth discussion of children and trauma is continued in Chapter 5.

Environmental disasters and trauma recovery

According to a paper published by the United Nations Office for Disaster Risk Reduction (UNISDR, 2012), there has been a significant increase in the number of people who live in flood-prone or cyclone/hurricane exposed areas. There were 4,130 disasters recorded between the years of 2002 and 2011; as a result of those disasters, 1,117,527 people lost their lives. The Centre for Research on the Epidemiology of Natural Disasters collects data on a natural disaster when at least one of the criteria below has been met:

•   ten or more people have been killed;
•   100 or more people have been affected by the event;
•   there has been a declaration of a state of emergency; and
•   there has been a call for international assistance.

Types of environmental disasters include earthquakes, volcanos, storms, floods, extreme drought, wildfires, insect infestations, and animal stampedes. In 2009, a total of 111 countries and 230.86 million people were affected by some sort of natural disaster. Of those people, 68.8 million were in

China alone (Vos, *et al.*, 2010). The risk of losing wealth in natural disasters now exceeds the rate at which wealth can be generated (UNISDR, 2012).

From a trauma-informed perspective, understanding the impact of these disasters goes far beyond loss of property and cannot be understood in economic terms alone. Understandably, the most vulnerable members of disaster-affected countries are most at risk and suffer the greatest. Studies on the impact of natural disasters on children reveal sleep disturbances (Brown, *et al.*, 2011), depression (Thienkrua, *et al.*, 2006), and anxiety-related disorders (La Greca, *et al.*, 2002; Thienkrua, *et al.*, 2006; Hensley-Maloney and Varela, 2009; Furr, *et al.*, 2010; Brown, *et al.*, 2011). For children, the cause of the disaster (i.e. environmental vs. man-made) matters less than their proximity to the disaster, their perception of the level of threat they or loved ones were in, or the death of a loved one (Furr, *et al.*, 2010). In December 2004, 20,000 children were affected by the devastating tsunami that struck Thailand. A study of 371 children who survived the tsunami was conducted by Thienkrua, *et al.* (2006) and revealed that 13 percent of children living in camps, and 11 percent living in villages demonstrated symptoms of PTSD. Additionally, 11 percent of the children in camps and 5 percent living in villages were experiencing symptoms of major depression. In a multivariate analysis, delayed evacuation, fear for their lives or the life of a loved one, and feelings of extreme fear were significantly associated with the symptoms of PTSD.

The impact of environmental disasters on adults can be financial, relational, emotional, and physical. The scope of these disasters results in losses of community resources and help, home destruction and job losses can economically devastate families (Mills, *et al.*, 2007; Madrid and Grant, 2008; Schumacher, *et al.*, 2010; Fernando and Hebert, 2011).

Despite the magnitude of the suffering mass disasters inflict, there was surprisingly little evidence-based literature related to best-practice methods to assist after a disaster. *Psychological Debriefing*, once considered the most desirable intervention following trauma exposure to reduce risk of developing PTSD, may not be effective in preventing symptoms after all; indeed, these interventions may actually be harmful to trauma survivors (Litz and Gray, 2002; McNally, *et al.*, 2003; Rose, *et al.*, 2003). After disasters, practitioners are thus left to their own education and training to do the best they can for survivors.

However, as we initially discussed in Chapter 1, intervention methods cannot necessarily be successfully be applied across cultures. Additionally, after a major disaster, there are simply not enough trauma-trained mental health professionals to offer treatment by traditional psychotherapeutic methods. In response to this need, Hobfoll, *et al.* (2007) collaborated and identified five essential elements of immediate and mid-term trauma intervention. The collaborators were well-published worldwide in the field of trauma and, from their analysis of trauma research, they identified the following principles to guide intervention:

1   *Promote a sense of safety.* Research reveals that both humans and animals require a sense of safety to reduce the neurobiological reaction brought on by threat, fear, or stress. Interventions related to promoting safety should include social support.
2   *Promote calming.* Trauma exposure causes a heightened level of arousal that, when prolonged, can interfere with sleep, lead to anxiety disorders, depression, and physical illness. The fear-circuitry response in the brain was meant for immediate survival; however prolonged activation of this system can cause long-term emotional and physical problems.
3   *Promote a sense of self-efficacy and collective efficacy.* Interventions should foster a sense that actions can lead to positive outcomes. After trauma, there is a risk that people may feel that they are not competent to handle what they must face. Collective efficacy refers to a group of people feeling that they are capable of accomplishing positive outcomes.
4   *Promotion of connectedness.* Based on a large body of evidence, globally, this principle highlights the importance that interventions foster the ability for trauma survivors to connect to loved ones. This need for connectedness and its positive role in trauma recovery has been identified across cultures.
5   *Instilling hope.* The literature on hope provides evidence that the ability to see a future that is more positive than the trauma-present appears to buffer the impact of trauma and promote well-being. This principle encourages interventions that identify and build upon the strengths of people at risk.

While there are not currently any clinical trials on the efficacy of the "five essential elements of immediate and mid-term mass trauma intervention," the authors' syntheses of the recurrent themes found within the trauma research is laudable. The five principles also offer guidelines that are portable across cultures and do not attempt to superimpose Western methods of treatment into other parts of the world. The five practice principles identified by Hobfoll, *et al.* (2007) are congruent with the symptom domains that we have identified from our review of the literature and are discussed in depth in Chapters 3 and 10.

Chapter 3

Neurobiology and the impact of trauma

One of the main objectives of this text was to provide a broad understanding of neuroscience research related to trauma, and then highlight how those findings can influence direct practice. Most practitioners who work with trauma survivors have neither the training, nor the interest, to conduct neurobiological studies; we leave that to the skills and talent of neurobiologists, neurochemists, and neuroanatomists. Over the past few decades the work of these scientists has helped identify some of the biological structures behind the complexity of symptoms we see related to trauma and recovery. Their labor helps us to make sense of our labor. We, as practitioners, have worked, or will work, with clients who exhibit many of the symptoms we will discuss in this and subsequent chapters. When we understand the neuroscience behind the symptoms, then what we see in practice begins to make sense. From a trauma-informed perspective, the behaviors that our clients present are actually *normal*. They may be maladaptive and disruptive, especially in children and adolescents, but they make sense scientifically. An exploration of the neurobiology of the brain's fear/stress response and the subsequent impact it has on neurochemical modulation provides a foundation for understanding the emotional, cognitive, and physical impact of trauma. With this knowledge, we can broaden our empathic understanding and further develop interventions that build upon neuroscience, and are not solely based on theoretical perspective.

Research on trauma draws heavily from early neuroscience studies on *stress*. Because safety is primary for the survival for any species, the brain constantly seeks information through the senses regarding environmental stressors. If something frightens us, the stress response in the brain is automatically triggered; thus within this context, fear, and stress are synonymous. However, persons with symptoms of PTSD may have more reactivity within the stress system than those persons who suffer from anxiety or stress (Yehuda, 2002). The neuroscience literature on stress provides a broad understanding of the microarchitectural impact of chronic stress on the brain, the physical risk factors that can develop because of chronic stress exposure, and the psychological and emotional consequences that can follow. As we will discover, chronic activation of this system can result in significant changes in how the brain interprets both internal and external cues. These changes within the brain contribute the symptoms that we see in treatment.

All animals have fear circuitry that promotes safety and survival. However, complexity of the human brain brings additional challenges; we feel and we think. As simple as that sounds, part of the challenge of trauma recovery in humans is the thinking/feeling part of the brain. The thinking/feeling part of the brain is "new" in the evolutionary process but still connected to the "old" part of the brain. This interplay between old and new brain functions appear to be at the root of trauma recovery. To explore this further, the goals for this chapter are twofold; to develop a basic understanding of neurobiological changes that can occur after trauma, and to understand the uniqueness related to interpretation of the trauma experience by each individual. Understanding both of these principles is essential in successful treatment with trauma survivors.

The function of the stress-response in the brain

Before the advances that have occurred in technology over the past several decades, we obtained much of what we assumed about the human brain by examining the organs of cadavers and by observing behavior (Kandel, 2000). However, thanks to neuroendocrine and neuroimaging technical advances, we now know that activity inside the brain is dependent largely on electrical and chemical interactions. While we are alive, what we sense, think, and fear, triggers electrical and chemical responses within the brain. These responses send messages that cause us to take action, affect our mood, affect our memory, and affect our ability to reason through problems. When we die, this brain activity ceases, as does our ability to measure it. In the past, postmortem examinations provided information on organ structure, but much of the function or purpose of these structures remained a mystery. Advances in neuroimaging technology over the past several decades have provided us with opportunities to be able to measure neurobiological and neurochemical responses in clients who are still living; this research has significantly broadened our understanding of trauma.

There is nothing abnormal about fear. The primary function of any organism's brain is survival (Sapolsky, 2004). The ability to sense threat and respond accordingly is essential. Without this ability to identify threat, any species, including humans, would become extinct. Therefore, an autonomic fear response is a primal function of any brain. We do not learn how to have this response; it happens automatically when the brain senses threat. Within this part of our brain, there are distinct systems that serve to regulate and evaluate information that we collect from our surroundings. Within the fear-circuitry system, the neuroendocrine function is important, and complex. This chemical arsenal is the first responder in times of threat.

Within seconds after a threat is first perceived by the brain, the sympathetic–adrenal–medullary (SAM) axis triggers a release of catecholamine, primarily norepinephrine, and epinephrine; also known as noradrenaline and adrenaline in Britain (Sapolsky, 2003, 2004). Within minutes following this chemical release, the hypothalamic–pituitary–adrenal (HPA) axis galvanizes to produce glucocorticoids (GCs), cortisol in humans (Sapolsky, *et al.*, 2000). The hypothalamus, which is about the size of the pea, serves as the control center to regulate body temperature, and send signals about being tired, hungry, thirsty, mad, or sad. It is also part of the limbic system, which serves as sort of an emotional highway for the brain (Perry, 2009; Carter, *et al.*, 2009). Also within this system is the amygdala, which processes, interprets, and integrates information provided by our senses. The amygdala is also where memories of fear are stored from experiences (LeDoux, 1996; Perry, 2001). The reason for the amygdala to retain these memories is, again, primal; the "old" brain needs to keep memories related to threat readily available for identification of a similar future threat. When receiving information through our senses, the amygdala determines what value that information should have, and then signal parts of the brain that control movement, heart rate, and blood pressure to respond accordingly (LeDoux and Phelps, 1993; LeDoux, 2012). The problem with this function appears to be the impact it has on other systems designed to determine context (time and place) of experiences. As we will see, when the amygdala is overactive, the "newer" parts of the brain become less active.

The stress response, while essential in times of threat, is designed to return to a baseline state when threat is no longer present (Yehuda and LeDoux, 2007). This process is known as *fear extinction*. When the autoregulation of the stress response system is dysfunctional, persons who experienced traumatic events in the past continue to experience heightened neurochemical reactions in the present without the existence of threat. The release of adrenaline facilitates the connection of threat memory and there is some evidence that failure to regulate the sympathetic nervous system response may lead to stronger encoding of a traumatic memory (McGaugh and Roozendaal, 2002). As we will see in subsequent chapters, the function of fear extinction is essential in trauma recovery. Without it, trauma survivors continue to exist in a heightened state of physiological arousal. When this occurs, we see behaviors and symptoms related to avoidance, hypervigilance, and exhaustion. Therefore, we can see that dysfunction in the regulatory processes related to fear extinction may be a root cause of posttraumatic symptom development.

Three major structures within the brain assist in regulating the stress response. They are: (a) the *hippocampus*; (b) the *amygdala*; and (c) the *prefrontal cortex* (Yehuda and LeDoux, 2007; Juster, *et al.*, 2011). The interplay between these three structures is complex and appears to be indicated in fear extinction, emotion regulation, and cognitive reasoning following trauma. These three structures also are interdependent for processing and storing memories. Memories, from a trauma-informed perspective, contribute to dysfunction when they are not processed into long-term memory. Adverse symptoms related to trauma memories involve context; context means the brain can differentiate between that past and the present in terms of threat.

In the short-term, stressors can enhance cognition; we can become focused and concentrate better under stress. However, in the long-term, chronic exposure to stress has the opposite effect and can disrupt cognitive reasoning. During times of stress, the adrenal steroid hormones, GCs are secreted to mobilize the body to fight or run (Sapolsky, 2003). There are numerous studies that indicate that prolonged exposure to GCs may be at the root of numerous physical and mental disorders such as diabetes, heart disease, anxiety, and depression (Sapolsky, *et al.*, 2000; Charney, 2004; Ganzel, *et al.*, 2010; Dhabhar, *et al.*, 2012).

There is some evidence that the hippocampus may be especially vulnerable to damage by exposure to prolonged stress (Brown, *et al.*, 1999; Schmahl, *et al.*, 2009; Carrión, *et al.*, 2010; Rao, *et al.*, 2010). The dysfunction in the hippocampus may contribute to several posttrauma symptoms. One important function of the hippocampus relates to memory and cognition. There are many theories within neuroscience related to the specific function of the hippocampus and processing memory (Bird and Burgess, 2008), but there appears to be general agreement that it does play a role. We create memories by experiences. These experiences develop into synaptic connections that create networks. Patterning creates stronger networks. When learning a task, we practice steps; these steps are part of explicit, or declarative memory. Over time, the patterning of these steps create strong neural nets within the brain and we no longer pay attention to each step while performing a task. At this point, the memory is implicit. Driving a car, riding a bike, or typing on a keyboard reaches a point that we are no longer conscious of the steps involved. Memories are important because they are perceptual. They relate to our understanding of experience. In trauma, memories of traumatic events can be intrusive; they do not haunt survivors from the past, they remain in the present. The hippocampus appears to play a role in the processing and storing of memories. Therefore, dysfunction in hippocampal functioning can contribute to memory intrusion (Peres, et al., 2008; Hayes, et al., 2010).

Early trauma-related neuroscience research revealed that persons with PTSD had smaller hippocampal volumes. There is some debate regarding whether hippocampal volumes are related to trauma exposure. There is a large body of research related to prolonged exposure to elevated stress hormones, such as cortisol, and hippocampal volume (Brown, et al., 1999; Hayes, et al., 2010; Rao, et al., 2010; McEwen, et al., 2012). Interesting twin research has revealed similar hippocampal volume in both combat-exposed and non-combat exposed twins (Gilbertson, et al., 2002) which may indicate that smaller hippocampal volume may be a vulnerability factor for developing PTSD rather than a result of exposure to traumatic events (Yehuda and LeDoux, 2007).

Regardless of the etiology of decreased hippocampal volume, the function, or dysfunction, of the hippocampus in trauma-related anxiety is important to understand. Another role of the hippocampus appears be the regulation of *context* of a threat, such as being able to distinguish between a picture of a bear and a live bear. A functioning hippocampus helps determine perspective and distinguish between safe and dangerous signals. Persons with posttrauma symptoms struggle with context. Non-threatening events that are similar to trauma reminders trigger behaviors so severe that they interfere with both social and occupational functioning. When this happens, the brain's ability to master context is evident. Persons with these symptoms experience the same fear reaction to a trigger that they would have to an actual threat.

The role of the amygdala in the stress response has become a focus of PTSD research in recent years and has been determined to be important in our understanding of PTSD (LeDoux, 1996; Yehuda and LeDoux, 2007). Activation in the amygdala occurs when threat stimuli are present. Studies using fMRI imaging have revealed that this activation occurs when conditioned (past experiences) and unconditioned threat cues are present (Sotres-Bayon, *et al.*, 2006; Kim, *et al.*, 2011). Whether a hyperactive amygdala pre-existed in persons with PTSD prior to traumatic events is currently unknown (Yehuda and LeDoux, 2007) and requires further research. At this time, it appears that hyperactivity in the amygdala inhibits fear extinction and the hippocampus from processing trauma memories (Hayes, *et al.*, 2010; El Khoury-Malhame, *et al.*, 2011; Kim, *et al.*, 2011). When the amygdala is overactive, it affects the functions of the prefrontal cortex (PFC) (Linnman, *et al.*, 2012).

Stress and fear cause the amygdala to be overactive. Fear extinction is dependent upon regulation from the PFC, and over-activation in the amygdala impedes the PFC from reasoning through experiences (Sotres-Bayon, *et al.*, 2004). The third region within the brain that appears to be vulnerable to trauma exposure is the PFC. In humans, the part of the evolutionary process that make our species unique is the development of a complex cortex. The cortex is the center for rational thought and helps determine meaning of an emotion or event (Sotres-Bayon, *et al.*, 2006). When a thought occurs, the cortex governs the quality and intensity of emotion related to that thought. Thoughts within the cortex are subjective, which explains why people can have different emotional responses to the same event. Malfunction in the PFC contributes to fear disorders, fear regulation, and hyperactivity in the amygdala (Yehuda and LeDoux, 2007). Conversely, hyperactivity in the amygdala inhibits the function of the PFC (Bush, *et al.*, 2007). Chronic exposure to fear impedes the ability of the PFC to rationally distinguish between past and present danger, think through problems, and determine solutions. When this occurs, the brain remains in a heightened, emotional state. It is believed that these three structures within the stress-response system play important roles in PTSD.

It should now be apparent why a general understanding of the stress response and fear circuitry within the brain is essential to a trauma-informed approach to care. Designed to prepare the body to fight a threat, or run from it, the initial flood of chemicals released by the stress-response system is essential for survival. Popularly known as "fight or flight," this response is part of the primary survival system. First coined by Walter Cannon in 1932, the model of "fight or flight" has become a standard way of understanding the fear response in both animals and humans (Taylor, *et al.*, 2000). While generally well accepted over the past 60 years, the concept of "fight or flight" may also be gender-biased. Research by Taylor, *et al.* (2000) determined that the majority of stress research from the years 1985– 2000 was conducted on male subjects, both human and animal. They argued that while aggressive behavior toward threat, or running from danger, may be adaptive for males, the same behavior may not be in the best interest of the females. Females, who may pregnant, nursing, or caring for offspring, would be highly vulnerable if fighting or running were their only natural responses to threat. If females are vulnerable, so is the survival of the entire species.

What Taylor and colleagues discovered in their research was that while both males and females experience the same initial chemical cascade at time of threat, there is evidence that there are significant other differences. Numerous studies have demonstrated increased testosterone levels in males under stress (Girdler, et al., 1997; Taylor, et al., 2000). This increased level of testosterone in males appears to be linked to the sympathetic arousal system (SAS) and is not solely activated for threat-related fight or flight response. Testosterone elevation also appears to be related to aggression and hostility, including rough-and-tumble play, not induced by threat (Girdler, et al., 1997). Unlike males, female aggression does not appear to be linked to the sympathetic arousal system (Taylor, et al., 2000).

Also not found to be dominant in the hierarchy of stress responses in females is the "flight" response. There may be an intrinsic biological rationale for this. Until fairly recently in the human continuum, females spent most of their adult life pregnant, nursing, or raising children. Given that these roles are central for the species to survive, running away from threat would not be feasible and would leave offspring vulnerable to danger. So if females have an intrinsic flight inhibition, and are not neurochemically predisposed to aggression, how have they survived over the millennia? It may be tempting to assume that female survival has been dependent on males, which enabled survival of both. However, while the "fight" response in males appears to be a dominant stress response, so does the "flight" response. Additionally, males who do not run from danger may not survive the battle with whatever threat is present. Therefore, the female stress system had to enable survival without male protection. But how? The answer to this evolutionary gender distinction may lie in the pituitary hormone oxytocin.

Oxytocin, a posterior pituitary hormone, released by both males and females during a broad range of stressors, may have a role in the female fear response and survival mechanism. Swedish physiology professor and worldwide authority on oxytocin, Kerstin Uvnäs Moberg, has published more than 400 scientific papers on the role of oxytocin. According to Uvnäs Moberg (1997, 2003) oxytocin appears to reduce fearfulness, decrease the "fight or flight" sympathetic response, and enhance relaxation.

Known as a "bonding" hormone, oxytocin fosters familial and social connections. Taylor, *et al.* (2000) propose that the oxytocin suppression of the fight or flight response encourages "tending" behavior in times of threat to protect offspring. Additionally, oxytocin may contribute to what Taylor, *et al.* refer to as "befriending" behavior. Group living in humans is viewed as an evolutionary adaptation that fosters safety. Individuals are safer from threat when part of a larger group. Under stress, females have more desire for social contact than males. Given this knowledge, it is feasible to explore trauma responses from gender-specific perspectives. Men and women are not the same. Future research specific research on gender differences in trauma may help us better understand appropriate treatment approaches that are mindful of the differences in stress responses.

The complex interaction of the entire stress response system is important to our understanding of trauma. Absence of fear extinction, emotion regulation, and cognitive distortions are the primary components that contribute to fear disorders.

The impact of chronic stress

Assessment for threat through external cues and our senses is constant (Carter, *et al.*, 2009). The processing of this information, first to determine if there is threat present, then for either long-term storage, or dismissed as not important, is how memories are created and learning occurs. Therefore, what we know and understand about our world is not merely observed, it is sensed. The brain's fundamental attempt to establish safety and balance occurs whether we want it to or not. The body's attempts to maintain a state of stable physiological balance, such as oxygen, acid levels, and body temperature is called *homeostasis*. Anything from the outside world that disrupts this state of balance is considered a *stressor*, and the *stress-response* is what the body attempts to do to re-establish homeostasis. In animals, the stress-response is usually triggered by an actual threat. The concept of homeostasis is grounded in biology, but this concepts has been expanded to include the multiple systems that respond and adapt to stressors over time. The expansion of the homeostatic concept is called *allostasis* (Korte, *et al.*, 2005; McEwen, 2008; McEwen, *et al.*, 2012). Within the framework of allostasis, the body is constantly trying to adapt to survive, not simply go back to an ideal homeostatic level. Under chronic stress, the constant activity of adaptation can cause wear and tear on the body, called *allostatic load* (AL). Over time, AL and chronic exposure to stress hormones can be more damaging to the body than the stressor itself (Korte, *et al.*, 2005;

McEwen, 2008; Liston, *et al.*, 2009). In other words, short-term activation of the stress-response keeps us alive, chronic activation makes us sick.

The physical impact of AL is well documented in the literature and associated with numerous negative physical consequences (Anda, *et al.*, 2006; Juster, *et al.*, 2011). The neuroscience concept of allostasis provides a framework that goes beyond the primal homeostatic balance of body temperature, energy, and blood composition because animals, including humans, are constantly interacting with their environments (Danese and McEwen, 2012). Allostasis refers to the ability to adapt to environmental threats by recognizing external and internal changes, and then activate the nervous, endocrine, and immune systems. Because the three systems are so highly integrated, activation in one system often triggers a response in the other two. This inter-related response is particularly evident during times of psychological or social stress.

Fear learning, avoidance behavior, and extinction (learning not to fear) are part of an adaptive system for managing a dangerous environment. The same normally adaptive system can cause harm, however, when fear becomes inappropriate in its signals and strength (Kirmayer, *et al.*, 2007). The amygdala is the region of the brain where conditioned fear is acquired. The prefrontal cortex is the brain region that inhibits the amygdala to retain fear, also called extinction. People diagnosed with PTSD, and other anxiety disorders, appear to have enhanced fear acquisition in the amygdala and delayed extinction (LeDoux, 2000). Fear arousal should trigger a state of alarm in the stress-response system of the brain that signals an autonomic endocrine response; a flood of neurochemicals designed for survival. Constant activation of the stress-response circuitry within the brain is unnatural. It may also lead to reactive and impulsive behavior (Ganzel, *et al.*, 2010; Rodrigues, *et al.*, 2009; Derryberry and Reed, 2002). Humans can activate this response simply by our thoughts (Sapolsky, 2004). And we often do.

In one of the first neuroimaging studies of PTSD, Rauch, *et al.* (1996) utilized script-driven imagery to evoke reminders of personal trauma in Vietnam combat veterans. When exposed to traumatic reminders, the study subjects had increases in cerebral blood flow to the right orbitofrontal cortex, insula, amygdala, and anterior temporal pole – all brain regions involved in the inhibition of intense emotions. There was decreased blood flow to the area known as Broca's area, which is considered the expressive speech center in the brain. These findings have led to similar studies that also support the perspective that traumatic reminders tend to decrease the ability to regulate intense emotions and interfere with the ability to translate experiences into expressive language (van der Kolk, 2006).

What makes us human

Much of the early fear study research was conducted on animals. These studies were, and continue to be, very enlightening on structural similarities common to humans and mammals. One of the complex systems implicated in trauma work is the limbic system. The limbic system, was largely ignored by neuroanatomists until Paul MacLean's groundbreaking research was published in 1949 (Lambert, 2003). In his work, entitled *Psychosomatic Disease and the 'Visceral' Brain*, MacLean departed from Broca's assertion that the limbic region was primarily olfactory and of little importance to humans. He instead proposed that mammalian brains may have a common primitive system for integrating information from senses, suggestive of a separation between intellectual behavior and emotional, nonverbal behavior (Lambert, 2003). MacLean continued to investigate the electrophysiological and anatomical aspects of the limbic cortex and its multiple associated sensory systems and, in 1969, proposed the concept of the *triune brain*. According to MacLean, humans have evolved to develop the cortex, while at the same time retaining two other primal functions. The oldest part of the brain, according to MacLean is *reptilian* (hindbrain), followed by the next evolutionary development, inherited from lower mammals, *the limbic system* (paleomammalian), and then finally the *neocortex* (neomammalian). The concept of the triune brain became very popular with the press and gained wide attention. This wide attention also fostered misconception; namely that humans have control over these three distinct brains, rather that each contributing to a single complex functioning brain. MacLean continued his research utilizing neuroimaging, and proposed evolutionary gender differences in humans, particularly the central role of mothers during the 180 million years of human evolution. MacLean's assignment of emotion to the limbic system began to be challenged when the role of the hippocampus was discovered to play a role in cognitive functioning and long-term memory (Lambert, 2003). Subsequent research indicates that emotions may be influenced by other systems as well. However, with lack of clarity regarding what those systems may be, MacLean's theory on emotions and the limbic system continue to be utilized, at least conceptually, in textbooks to this day.

The impact of MacLean's concept of the limbic system was so well articulated that, according to LeDoux (2000), many researchers believed the mystery of how the brain creates emotions appeared to have been solved. During this time, research energy was diverted to cognitive studies. As a result, there has been a gap in the neuroscience research related to the emotional response circuitry over the past few decades (LeDoux, 2000).

However, interest in the fear circuitry within the brain appears to have generated new interest in research on the emotional brain.

It is emotional complexity and the ability of the neocortex to integrate a variety of different sources of information, attach meaning to information, and apply logical thought as to how to respond to the information that makes humans different from other species in the animal kingdom (van der Kolk, 2006). However, as we will discuss further in Chapters 5 and 6, this ability to apply reason to experiences can be thwarted by chronic exposure to trauma. Feelings of helplessness, the inability to escape, and chronic fear can cause long-term damage in the emotion-regulating systems in the brain and impede the ability to apply logical thought to the intense emotions traumatic memories evoke (LeDoux, 2000; van der Kolk, 2006).

Implications for direct practice

Studied more than other trauma-related syndromes, PTSD dominates the field of trauma research. PTSD occurs in 10 to 25 percent of trauma survivors (Kessler, et al., 1995), however most trauma survivors do not meet the full diagnostic criteria defined by the DSM-IV-TR (American Psychiatric Association, 2000). Persons with PTSD experience symptoms clustered into three co-occurring groups:

- re-experiencing symptoms
- avoidance symptoms
- hyperarousal symptoms.

While most trauma survivors experience many of these symptoms immediately following a traumatic event, most experience a decline in distress within three months (Kessler, et al., 1995). This provides us with a normative picture of fear extinction and the ability to return to a non-threat state. Persons with prolonged symptoms, or those who develop them long after an event occurred, provide evidence that there are biological mechanisms that are dysfunctional and impede recovery (Yehuda and LeDoux, 2007). Therefore traditional treatment strategies that may work with many other clients may be ineffective with this population.

A discussion of the application of neuroscience to direct practice contains some inherent challenges. First, there is not a universally accepted consensus, even among neuroscientists, on absolute specific regions of the brain that are affected by trauma. Additionally, most traditional treatment in mental health is grounded in theory. Some of these theoretical perspectives appear dated in light of recent neuroscience data. Despite these challenges, there is little doubt that neuroscience research has provided insight into specific targets that can be used for developing trauma-informed approaches to care.

Most of the treatment approaches presented in Chapters 5, 6, 7, and 8 were either developed, or adapted, for trauma-specific treatment. While it has been common to utilize traditional talk-therapy to treat trauma survivors in the past, there is little evidence in the research of its effectiveness. Neuroimaging findings reveal that the higher brain areas that manage rational thought become less active under stress (van der Kolk, 2006). Therefore, traditional talk-therapy may elicit strong emotional responses while the client relates their experience, but they may lack the ability to integrate emotion and cognition by talking alone.

In the following chapters, our review of the literature identified four distinct areas of posttrauma functioning that appear to be common areas of distress for trauma survivors. They are dysfunction in fear extinction, emotion regulation, attentional bias and cognitive distortions, and relational issues. Each of these areas appear to be interconnected and cause distinct distress to trauma survivors who develop adverse posttrauma symptoms. In Chapter 10, we offer suggestions how to integrate understanding about each of these four areas in order to promote trauma-informed services.

Fear extinction

As noted earlier in this chapter, fear extinction is the ability to return to a state of calm following threat. Fear extinction is one of the areas identified as at-risk following prolonged stressors. Dysfunction in the fear circuitry in the brain and fear extinction has been associated with anxiety disorders, including PTSD (Graham and Milad, 2011; Sehlmeyer, et al., 2011). While physicians commonly treat anxiety using medications, such as benzodiazepines and selective serotonin reuptake inhibitors (SSRIs), there is no indication that medications are curative. Cognitive behavior therapy (CBT) is generally the treatment of choice for anxiety disorders, including PTSD, and often include "exposure" strategies that do precisely that; expose a client, over time, to the feared activity or object while employing cognitive techniques to reassure safety (McNally, 2007; Hofmann and Smits, 2008).

The systems involved in fear extinction include interaction between the prefrontal cortex, the amygdala, and the hippocampus. When extinction occurs, threat is experienced in context. For instance, a near accident elicits a neurochemical flood, heightened alertness, and a physiological response in preparation for action. When that event is over, heart rate, blood pressure, and stress hormones return to a baseline state. Part of this process involves the hippocampus in determining context (now vs. then) and the prefrontal cortex processing the event (Sapolsky, 2004; Corcoran, 2005). While, this occurs, the amygdala activation decreases. In clients with PTSD, these systems appear to have adapted to a chronic perception of fear that inhibits fear extinction. Prolonged exposure to threat creates a *conditioned* fear response, where the brain attempts to anticipate the next threatening event, despite the fact that real threat no longer exists. Numerous studies demonstrate heightened amygdala activity and diminished activity in the prefrontal cortex in persons with conditioned fear (Sotres-Bayon, *et al.*, 2006; Sehlmeyer, *et al.*, 2011; Linnman, *et al.*, 2012). When this occurs, the amygdala is hyper-responsive and cognitive control becomes inadequate to mediate this hyperemotional response (Tamminga, 2006; Sotres-Bayon, 2008; Amanao, *et al.*, 2010). Dysfunction in the neural circuitry related to fear extinction cause long-term distress for trauma survivors as evidenced by hypervigilance, hyperarousal, sleep disturbances, and avoidance behaviors. While there is strong evidence that dysfunction in the fear extinction circuitry is problematic for trauma survivors, often it is overlooked in treatment. Because of the primacy of function of safety in the brain, understanding the role of fear extinction is essential in treating the long-term impact of trauma.

Emotion regulation

As we have noted, hyperactivity in the amygdala region in response to trauma cues inhibits activity in the prefrontal cortex (Banks, *et al.*, 2007). Emotion regulation is a common area of distress for both child and adult survivors of trauma. Behaviors such as impulsivity, depression, anxiety, and rage are well documented in trauma literature (Foa and Kozak, 1986; Banks, *et al.*, 2007; Goldin, *et al.*, 2009; Kim, *et al.*, 2011; LeDoux, 2012). Difficulty with emotion regulation causes distress in relationships and occupational functioning. According to our interpretation of the neuroscience literature, emotion regulation is intertwined with fear extinction. Therefore, promoting a sense of calm and safety contributes to the ability of the PFC to regulate emotion.

Attentional bias and cognitive distortions

When applied to trauma survivors, the term *attentional bias* refers to the detection of threat stimuli, difficulty in disengaging with trauma cues, and attentional avoidance away from trauma reminders (Cisler, *et al.*, 2009; Blair, *et al.*, 2013). Attentional bias has been observed at higher rates in persons with anxiety disorders and is typically not observed in persons without anxiety. Research demonstrates that anxious individuals display attentional bias toward threatening sources of information, a behavior not observed in non-anxious individuals. A review of 172 research studies revealed compelling evidence of attentional bias toward threatening stimuli, difficulty disengaging from threatening stimuli, or both in most anxious participants (Bar-Haim, *et al.*, 2007). There is some indication attentional bias may be both automatic and strategic, and influenced by the amount of time that has passed since the initial fear stimulus occurred (Cisler, *et al.*, 2009). The clinical implications of attentional bias relate to cognitive control and disengaging from traumatic cues (Blair, *et al.*, 2013). Attentional bias is an emotional response and interferes with problem-solving and rational thought. Amygdala over-activity in the presence of attentional bias mirrors the systems dysfunction noted in the absence of fear extinction; there is a hyperfocus on threat cues and a decrease in cortico-limbic functioning (El Khoury-Malhame, *et al.*, 2011).

Attentional control is a cognitive process that can help regulate attentional bias (Derryberry and Reed, 2002). Hyperactivation of the amygdala inhibits activation in the prefrontal cortex, thus interfering with problem-solving and contextual understanding. Memories may be intrusive because the hippocampus is affected by heightened amygdala activity (Hayes, *et al.*, 2010) and distorted counterfactual thinking may occur (Branscombe, *et al.*, 2003). Strategies that integrate safety – which is essential for fear extinction, target reduction of attentional bias, and addresses cognitive distortions – appear to be most efficacious in treating trauma survivors.

Relationships and trauma

Disruptions and dysfunctions in human relationships can be one of the long-lasting scars left by traumatic events. Sadly, supportive relationships are also identified as an important aspect of trauma recovery (Hobfoll, *et al.*, 2007). Trauma experienced in childhood can interfere with the natural ability to form bonds with others (Bowlby, 1988; Bornstein, 2005; Fraser, *et al.*, 2010). Relationships and social support are identified as extremely important in trauma recovery for children, adult survivors of childhood trauma, survivors of natural disasters, and military veterans. As we will explore in later chapters, relationships can either hinder or contribute to resilience, coping, and recovery. Many of the treatment methods considered "trauma-informed" foster symptom reduction that may contribute to relational improvements. However, we encourage the focus on relationships not to be simply an outcome to treatment. As we explore trauma-informed practice in the remaining chapters of this book, the need for relationship support will become more evident. Humans are social creatures and do not live their lives in isolation. Therefore, treatment with a focus on individual pathology without addressing environmental support becomes irrelevant.

Chapter 4

Resilience and trauma recovery

Essential to any trauma work is the process of developing a relationship of trust with the client. Few would argue that successful outcomes begin with this important step. However, there was little data on the efficacy of support therapy alone for treating trauma survivors. While generally all practitioners may understand the power of establishing a safe environment for the client, there is probably no population of clients within our scope of practice where the construct of safety is more crucial. Because of the brain's primal need for safety, this is one of the most important components of any trauma-informed approach. Additionally, properly assessing the individual needs of each client, and determining which intervention may be feasible, and acceptable, to the client, their culture, and their setting is crucial to keeping the focus on the whole individual and not just the trauma symptoms evidence-based.

The challenge of this chapter was to identify treatment methods that foster resilience for victims of trauma. The definition of resilience may vary significantly from culture to culture but we attempt to define the concept based on existing research and data from neuroscience studies. As discussed in Chapter 1, the stigma of having symptoms of mental health problems can be significant in some cultures and a barrier to service. That barrier expands significantly if treatment methods, which may be widely accepted in one culture, are superimposed onto trauma victims in a different culture without consideration of existing norms and values. It is important, therefore, for practitioners to assist victims of violence to define their own conceptual framework for recovery within the context of their own culture and community.

However, as noted in Chapter 1, most of the literature that is published in the field of mental health comes out of developed, resource abundant, countries that approach trauma recovery from a specialist perspective.

Candidly, both authors of this text are trained as clinical social workers in the United States and fall within that specialist criteria. But the concept of trauma-informed care lends itself well to breaking this paradigm and offers an opportunity to think more broadly about the application of treatment. The basics of neuroscience discussed in Chapter 3 generally, and Chapters 5, 6, 7, and 8 in population-specific terms, help us better understand why some of the evidence-based treatments provided in this chapter may have the outcomes that they do.

It may be difficult for someone from a developed nation to understand how a person, who may live in a remote village without access to psychiatrists, psychologists, clinical social workers, and psychotropic medications, still recovers from a traumatic event. We have already acknowledged that the vast majority of trauma research comes out of developed countries. We have also acknowledged that this may skew our understanding of trauma recovery. Therefore, in this chapter, we provide conceptual information that may help us understand the variables related to trauma recovery by exploring the concept of resilience from a theoretical and neurobiological perspective. This combined approach may help us make sense of some of the barriers and successes in trauma treatment from a larger viewpoint. While explored in more detail in Chapters 5 and 6, we also begin a discussion on *attachment* in this chapter. A base understanding of attachment, from both a theoretical and neurobiological perspective, is important in understanding barriers to resilience. The concepts of hope and self-perception are two of the main constructs found in attachment, cognitive restructuring, and resilience theories. This chapter provides the reader with a meta-analysis of research that demonstrates the efficacy of these theories as a framework for assessment and intervention in working with survivors of trauma. The rationale for choosing these particular theories are twofold: there is substantial literature demonstrating positive treatment outcomes for trauma recovery from these intervention perspectives, and the pivotal theoretical constructs that ground these theories are congruent with our findings in the neurobiological literature.

With the challenge of cultural relativity already established, the focus on resilience and attachment in this chapter was determined by the following benchmarks:

- evidence of efficacy
- cultural portability
- practitioner adaptability.

For the purposes of this book, *evidence of efficacy* refers to a body of literature that demonstrates that resilience and attachment treatment has resulted in measurable outcomes across populations. Because a client's internal perception is so embedded in the theoretical perspective of resilience, we expand our review of the literature to include treatment methods that utilize a cognitive approach. Our benchmark of *cultural portability* encouraged us to examine methods of treatment that have demonstrated efficacy in varying cultures, and/or have qualities that could be modified to be useful within varying cultural norms. *Practitioner adaptability* references awareness that the existence of, and reliance upon, postgraduate trained psychotherapists may not the norm in many countries and cultures. Therefore, we have attempted to identify interventions that have both a clinical and broader focus. Broadening the treatment perspective for trauma is supported by data emerging from neuroscientists and furthers the applicability of trauma-informed care.

Resilience: origins and definitions

A review of the resilience literature revealed that there were varying definitions of resilience and debate regarding application of the concept as it relates to trauma. It is also quite dated. There is no universally accepted definition of resilience, which has implications for accepting research findings in a comparative fashion (Luther, *et al.*, 2000). Children have been the focus of much of the resilience research, which we will discuss further in Chapter 5. There is some debate on whether resilience should be viewed as a personal trait or a process (Luther, *et al.*, 2000). This discussion has implications for practice; our intervention would vary depending on how we perceive resilience. If resilience is a trait, how much can be done to influence an individual's personality? If resilience it is a process, which treatment approach best fosters the capacity for resilience? Luther, *et al.* (2000) propose that future research more clearly differentiate between the two concepts. They argue that the term *resiliency* be used when describing traits as it describes personality characteristics of an individual who may, or may not, have experienced adversity. *Resilience*, however, should be used when referring to the developmental process of maintaining positive adaptation in the face of adverse life circumstances.

Within the resilience literature, the implied definition of resilience is person's capacity to experience a traumatic event and have little, or no, injurious effects in the aftermath (Harvey, 2007). Indeed, many trauma survivors demonstrate what is called "positive" or "adversarial growth" in subsequent years as a result of their trauma experience. Harvey (1996) encourages a multidimensional perspective that discards an "all or nothing" approach to resilience and understands that a person may appear to thrive posttrauma but still be suffering. Within this perspective, resilience can be co-occurring with distress.

Charney (2004) recommends an integrated model of resilience that would include adaptive neurobiological factors that help control the stress response. He encourages practitioners to examine which treatment methods would help develop or strengthen stress–related adaptive neurobiological factors. According to Charney, trauma survivors who demonstrate resiliency after the trauma event appear to have ample prefrontal cortex ability to reduce amygdala excitation. In other words, they have the neurobiological ability to calm themselves down. This neurobiological information can help practitioners focus interventions that strategically target specific brain circuitry.

As noted in the discussion of personal trauma in Chapter 2, there is no universal treatment approach to trauma recovery; trauma survivors each bring their own uniqueness to their trauma experience. Self-perception, coping strategies, and the client's perception of the meaning of the trauma present a complex interplay of variables that require practitioners to develop their trauma assessment skills as competently as their intervention skills. Indeed, given the complex nature of human recovery, assessment should be an ongoing process.

As noted in Chapter 3, there is extensive literature that attempts to provide insight regarding the biological and environmental processes that affect a person's perception and understanding of the world around them. Recovery from trauma is never quick, easy, or guaranteed. However, generally individuals will, naturally, attempt to find a sense of balance, or homeostasis, after the exposure to a traumatic event has subsided. Research has determined several individual components that support recovery (Funk, 1992; Eisold, 2005; Friborg, et al., 2009; Gilman, et al., 2012). These components include:

- resilience
- hardiness and coping
- developmental maturity
- attachment
- posttraumatic growth.

As practitioners, we know that the strengths that an individual possesses are the building blocks for their pathway to return to a sense of homeostasis. With trauma, there are many components of one's developmental status and emotional experiences that will either promote, or interfere with, their recovery. The historical roots of the concept of resilience are commonly attributed to sociologist Aaron Antonovsky (McSherry and Holm, 1994; Breed, et al., 2006; Lindström and Eriksson, 2006; Morrison and Clift, 2006). Antonovsky (1987) coined the term *salutogenesis*; a derivation of Latin *salus*, meaning health and the Greek term *genesis* meaning beginning. Antonovsky became interested in exploring what creates health, rather than what creates pathology, while he was conducting research on the health of a group of women who were World War II Holocaust survivors. The concept of salutogenesis focuses on three characteristics:

1   Finding solutions and problem-solving
2   Identifies resources that help someone move toward positive health
3   Identifies the capacity, or *sense of coherence* (SOC) for this process
(Antonovsky, 1987).

SOC is determined by personal elements of cognition, behavior, and motivation that determine a person's ability to address, or resolve, current event(s) by utilizing personal and community resources in a proactive manner. It is one's ability to manage their environment fosters their health and mental health (McSherry and Holm, 1995; Eriksson and Lindström, 2005; Morrison and Clift, 2006). When examining a person's SOC, the focus is not on the problem and how to resolve problem-related barriers. Instead, the focus is upon a person's ability to find solutions. The integration of the person's social and environmental resources along with one's cognition, behavior, and motivation to recover provide the individual, or community, a sense of coherence.

To measure SOC, Antonovsky (1993) developed the Sense of Coherence Scale. The scale has several versions; the earliest version contains 29 items, a 13-item version has also been used. Since its creation, the SOC questionnaire has been translated into at least 33 different languages and has been used in 32 countries in Europe, South Africa, Thailand, China, and Japan (Sardu, et al., 2012). Because of the focus on well-being, rather than pathology, the instrument appears to provide a method for cross-cultural applicability in assessing health and well-being.

The concept of salutogenics and a sense of coherence provide a foundation for the theory of resilience. Much of the literature defines resilience from a positive perspective. Historically, the public, and the professional community, have viewed a traumatic situation from a problem-related framework. What is wrong, what are the barriers to recovery, and what strategies do we need to utilize to address the problem? But that approach changes when looking at an adverse situation from a resilience perspective, the question becomes "how does a person rise up and look beyond any barrier, or adversity, with a sense of purpose?" A person with this display of confidence will bend and engage in a positive adaptation to their negative circumstance (Masten, 2001).

Resilience is experienced when an individual displays self-confidence, independence, and self-control as they make decisions to their benefit. Scheier and Carver (1985) refer to this as one's ability to be optimistic versus the person who is pessimistic. A resilient person utilizes coping strategies to support themselves in the process of recovery from their trauma(s). For the practitioner, this requires the ability to identify a client's strength that supports their recovery. The practitioner will focus on what is working for the individual at this time, assist them in identifying those strengths, and work collaboratively to further support the recovery process into the future. Assessment of a client's functioning from a resilience perspective focuses upon what is going well for the individual, their strengths, such as cognitive knowledge and self-esteem, their use of personal and community resources, and a view of the immediate or anticipated situation in a comprehensible manner. Mak, *et al.* (2011) recognize cognitive theorist, Aaron Beck (2008) for conceptualizing that depressed individuals develop a *negative cognitive triad* where they view themselves, their world, and their future in negative terms. Mak, *et al.* proposed that resilient people have developed a *positive cognitive triad* which enables a view of themselves, their world, and their future from a positive perspective. In a study of 1,419 Chinese young adults, resilience appears to be significantly related to a person's positive cognitive triad. The researchers recommend that strategies to foster a positive cognitive triad should be developed and explored to assist in fostering resilience (Mak, *et al.*, 2011).

However, an understanding of resilience should not come from an "all or nothing" perspective. Bonanno (2004) argues that there are multiple pathways to resilience and that resilience is different from recovery. Bonanno posits that recovery suggests that, after a trauma, a person experiences disruption in their normal functioning, such as anxiety or depression, and then eventually returns to a state of base functioning: they have recovered. Resilience refers to a person's ability to maintain a sense of stability despite adverse experiences. However, resilience should not be understood as simply the absence of pathology (Bonanno, 2004). Bonanno argues that resilience is common; it is the Western parts of the world's assumption that trauma and grief require professional intervention. A person who has the ability to be flexible, even while experiencing anxiety or depression, is considered resilient (Montpetit, et al., 2010). According to Ong, et al. (2006), a person's ability to experience positive emotions within the context of stress is adaptive. Therefore, interventions should promote an individual's capacity to experience emotional complexity during times of stress and to benefit from the ability to remain positive in times of adversity. For the resilient individual, positive emotions are more common. The individual who has difficulty in rebounding after a traumatic or stressful event is more negatively reactive to such an event. Resilient individuals can move toward improved personal development after a traumatic experience, but may also remain susceptible in some areas of their development. While they may resume their everyday life, they may question particular values they once held such as, personal faith, the institution of marriage, and personal relationships. For example, if one experiences a sense of shame, it can influence furthering relationships in a desired manner, lessen one's self-esteem and diminish their self-confidence (Tedeschi and Kilmer, 2005; Van Vliet, 2008). If an individual suffers from depression and anxiety and then faces a traumatic event, or stressor, they may be able to utilize prior positive experiences to offset a negative response to what is occurring (Zuatra, et al., 2001; Tedeschi and Kilmer, 2005).

Social workers and social psychologists have long held the perspective that individual well-being cannot be understood without acknowledgment of the interconnection of a person to their social environment. Understanding resilience from this perspective, a practitioner can assist clients to draw not only from their internal strengths, but from their social resources as well.

Hardiness and coping

Within the resilience literature, *hardiness* refers to personality traits that support rebalancing after a traumatic experience. A person displays hardiness by their ability to commit to their life, and be in control of their destiny when facing a challenge (Bartone, et al., 1989; Funk, 1992). In other words, persons considered "hardy" have a firm and focused belief that they can control either their experience of an event, the event itself, or both. What seems to fuel this belief is a sense of excitement to the challenge they face; as if to say, "I am able to do this no matter what." The experience is balanced by this excitement and the individual's sense of personal commitment to his or her own life. Early research on the concept of hardiness has been correlated to sustained health even after the experience of a traumatic event (Bartone, *et al.*, 1989; Clark and Hartman, 1996).

Coping after an adversity reflects a process of adaptation rather than a personality trait. While the difference may appear subtle, from a practitioner perspective it is profound. When working with a person who has experienced trauma, we need to determine whether we are attempting to build upon an individual's base personality traits of hardiness, or to help a client develop process strategies to cope. Coping involves drawing upon cognitive resources to develop strategies to adapt to adverse life situations. However, understanding how the trauma may have affected a person's capacity for this cognitive process is at the root of a trauma-informed approach. Because of the neural responses to fear, this process can be compromised on a level that reaches beyond cognition.

Research on the fear circuitry of the brain explores the processes that occur in order to return, physiologically, to a baseline state of calm (Emanuel, 2004; Rodrigues, *et al.*, 2009). Generally, when confronted with a life stressor, we are able to think through a situation and find a way to cope. This ability to "think through" a problem can be compromised after experiencing trauma. Research on *fear extinction* – the capacity to return to a baseline sense of calm after threat – reveals that, after chronic stressors, the ability of the prefrontal cortex to determine that a threat no longer exists may be compromised by other regions in the brain (Rogan, *et al.*, 1997; Sotres-Bayon, *et al.*, 2006; Rodrigues, *et al.*, 2009). As discussed in Chapter 3, this region of the brain is designed for survival, not chronic activation. Exposure to threat can disrupt the circuitry involved in fear extinction, which compromises emotion regulation, impulse control, and cognitive process (Koenen, *et al.*, 2001; Briere, *et al.*, 2008).

The ability to adapt, reason through problems, and develop strategies is fundamental coping skills. These rational and largely non-emotional activities draw heavily upon the prefrontal cortex – the executive center – within the brain. A study to evaluate cognitive deficits of veterans with PTSD compared to a control group without PTSD indicated that hyperactivity of the limbic system might contribute to prefrontal cortical dysfunction (Koenen, *et al.*, 2001).

Knowledge of the possible disruption in the capacity for coping and problem-solving that may be experienced by trauma survivors provides opportunities for different strategies for practitioners. Developing alternate means of coping, or coping flexibility, may assist clients with establishing patterned, behavioral, alternatives to thinking through a problem which may enhance their coping capacity (Bonanno, 2004; Bonanno, *et al.*, 2005; Coifman, *et al.*, 2007; Westphal, *et al.*, 2008). There is some research that demonstrates a positive correlation with coping flexibility, hardiness, and a reduction of posttraumatic stress (Bonnano, *et al.*, 2011).

For the treating practitioner, the concept of coping flexibility may be viewed as synonymous with the positive cognitive triad of resilience in the recovery process. Thus the treatment focus is upon the person's cognitive, emotional, social and other environmental supports and strengths to support and empower the forward view of a positive future beyond the trauma. While there is substantial data on the efficacy of creating a safe environment where a person can re-experience, and retell, their traumatic experience, the concept of coping flexibility may offer an alternative mechanism for a trauma survivor to move beyond their past experience (Coifman, *et al.*, 2007).

Developmental maturity

The impact of trauma on development will be discussed in depth in Chapters 5 and 6. There is extensive research that indicates that one's ability to be resilient may be grounded in early life development. How our caregivers managed adverse child experiences may set the path for how we cope, regulate, and manage similar situations today. Leipold and Greve (2009) state that an individual's successful development relies upon an ability to maintain, regulate, and adapt to a challenging situation. Eisenberg and Silver (2011) agree and state that a child's ability to regulate the intensity of their emotions, and how their emotions are expressed, largely depends upon how they were raised. However, neuroscience provides us with a better understanding as to why this occurs; emotion regulation is more complex than simply thinking positive thoughts.

Research on the stress response in the brain reveals that sensing threat can automatically stimulate the secretion of hormones that are designed for survival. Sensing threat can be as simple as reminders of past events that were perceived as dangerous. One of the ways scientists study this phenomenon is to examine fear conditioning. Studies on fear conditioning may better help us understand why some people are able to return to a baseline alert state, while others remain in a physiological and emotional state of threat alert. One of the PTSD criteria is the symptom of hyperarousal. As we have discussed in previous chapters, the chronic arousal of the fear circuitry in the brain can lead to a myriad of health and mental health issues. In the past, much of what we understand about fear conditioning was derived from animal studies (Sapolsky, *et al.*, 2000; Rudy, *et al.*, 2004). As we noted in

Chapter 3, neurons change by activity; patterned activity creates neural networks. When this activity is chaotic and unpredictable during the early years of life, the neural systems in children attempt to adapt to this constant threat; while this adaptation within the neural networks make sense biologically, the results can cause long-term problems for the child. However, as we will discuss in the next chapter, children appear to be able to "re-wire" the patterns caused by early experiences when there is stability in their environments and relationships (Perry and Hambrick, 2008).

Hope

The concept of hope has been tangentially defined as an ability to think and define pathways toward a desired goal, as well as being able, and motivated, to use these pathways to attain that goal (Snyder, 2002; Irving, *et al.*, 2004). It has further been defined in terms of a trilogy of goals, pathways, and agency referring to one's perceived capacity to accomplish a goal (Snyder, *et al.*, 1991). Importantly, and of value, to trauma–informed care providers, the concept of hope may be an important component of an overarching ability to be resilient during and beyond a traumatic event(s).

Snyder (2002) describes the component of goals as a mental target which may, or may, not include a visual image. Goals can be either short term (I am leaving for the store in the next ten minutes), or long term (I plan to purchase a home in two years). They can be positive (buying a home) or negative meaning to deter or put something off (I will not gain ten pounds while cruising the Mediterranean Sea). In either case, goals are somewhat uncertain. Yet a person with hope reflects upon their motivation and capacity (agency) to reach that desired end. Pathways involve the ability to identify a plan or avenue that will take them toward a goal. While a pathway may not involve a visual image it could also be described as a roadmap; a route to follow so as not to get lost on the way toward a desired goal. Irving, *et al.* (2004) have defined a pathway as a route around a problem.

The understanding of *agency* involves self-assessment of one's ability to attain the goals by way of the pathways (Snyder, 2002). Bandura refers to agency as ability in terms of *self-efficacy*, which refers to one's belief that one has the ability to create and manage events in one's life (Bandura, 1982, 1997; Irving, *et al.*, 2004; Gilman, *et al.*, 2012). Hope plays an integral role in motivation for growth beyond trauma. The ability to have hope draws upon cognitive functioning, social resources, spiritual beliefs, and behavioral abilities. Hope assists with moving beyond the effects of trauma to a predictive environment.

Attachment

The fundamental premise of Attachment Theory relates to the human need to form deep emotional attachments with another. John Bowlby, the pioneer of Attachment Theory, conducted numerous studies on the severe emotional distress observed in children when separated from their parent, usually a mother (Bowlby, 1954, 1970, 1988; Bowlby, et al., 1956). Levy, et al. (2010) further define the role of attachment for adults as providing a base for safety, and comfort in times of distress. This basic need to feel safe is congruent with what we have already discussed related to the primal needs of the human brain. As most mammals are social creatures, safety would include social bonds.

In childhood, attachment figures can be a parent, guardian, or a person who helps us feel safe. As we get older, attachments can be formed in a romantic relationship. This emotional bonding and nurturing relationship fosters confidence as we develop an understanding of our environment. As children interact with their environment, they recognize they have support and encouragement from a significant attachment figure. Within the construct of Attachment Theory, *secure attachment* is demonstrated when there is a strong degree of trust that serves as the basis for a committed and engaged relationship. The person with a secured attachment is more likely to be independent within their environment while able to further themselves with knowledge to add to their self-confidence and decision-making abilities. According to Bowlby's theory, children can also develop *insecure attachment* when a caregiver is unpredictable. Children who experience this often feel unloved or unworthy and may struggle with this feeling into adulthood. Exposure to trauma in childhood can result in what is referred to as *disorganized attachment*. Disorganized attachment, according to Attachment Theory, can cause difficulties with mood regulation, impulse control, and cognitive impairments. Children who experience childhood trauma may exhibit these behaviors, and in the next chapter we will explore further some of the neuroscience rationale for why.

Bartholomew and Horowitz (1991) propose that adults may demonstrate *preoccupied attachment*, where they often view others as better off than they, become over-involved in relationships, and are dependent upon others for approval and self-worth. A person with preoccupied attachment may be viewed as social and engaging, eager and motivated to learn more of how to improve their relationships with others and throughout their environment. They can be viewed as pleasers who eventually become disappointed in the relationship and distance themselves away. The person with *dismissing attachment* presents as being aloof of emotional relationships, shallow, guarded in emotional display, states a need to be independent of others, retreats from assistance of others and is often confused by their emotions (Ainsworth, 1989; Levy, *et al.*, 2010). Lastly, *unresolved attachment* for trauma and loss attachment refers to those individuals who have experienced childhood traumas, including sexual, physical, and emotional, which may increase their susceptibility to ongoing abuse as an adult. Persons with unresolved attachment may develop mental health disorders such as PTSD, depression, and anxiety (Alexander, 2009; Levy, *et al.*, 2010). The person with unresolved attachment due to trauma and loss often experiences shame, feelings of insecurity, low self-esteem, dependency, and limited ability to trust (Ainsworth, 1989; Alexander, 2009).

Whether a practitioner ascribes to the contextual terms defined by various attachment theorists, there is little dispute regarding the underscoring assumption: humans have an intrinsic need to bond in order to feel safe. The professional community has accepted the theory that the style of attachment to a nurturing figure has an influence upon one's ability to navigate one's adult life and the quality that it brings. Clinically, the implications of the style of one's attachment to a figure as a secure base will determine the treatment interventions for many individuals and the success of treatment will often vary.

Posttraumatic growth

While resilient individuals can move toward improved personal development after trauma, there can be the possibility that they remain susceptible in some developmental areas. While one may resume an everyday lifestyle, one may question particular values once held such as personal faith, institutions of marriage, and personal relationships, as examples. What occurs for those who rebound from trauma, those who move forward in a fluid and adaptable manner? Some of what is involved in this phenomenon are protective factors leading to posttraumatic growth.

Of interest to the attestation of individual resilience is the construct of personal protective factors. The construct explains one's ability to make connections with others and be resilient when also faced with adversity. The concept posits that the beginnings of these factors are developed in infancy and childhood. The extensions of these abilities include knowing that one is safe with others. Protective factors include empathy, personality style, social supports, communication (including engaging in relationships with others) flexibility in a new encounter perceived or unexpected, problem–solving, and dispositional resilience. These constructs uphold an individual's positive self-regard (Eisold, 2005; Friborg, *et al.*, 2009; Montpetit, *et al.*, 2010).

Dispositional resilience refers to the uniqueness of an individual in which they regard careers and work in general, while feeling in control of their direct environment and willing to take on future challenges and new encounters. It is also referred to as hardiness (Bartone, *et al.*, 2009). Social supports refer to emotional regard and connection with family, friends, and colleagues. It also refers to the interpersonal supports found in one's place of worship, community groups of mutual interests and state and national organizational memberships pertaining to career and personal pursuits.

Communication is a broad term, but in this area refers to the manner that one is able to listen to others, express their thoughts so as to gain information to be utilized in a manner to promote their welfare and experience. One's ability to be flexible refers to adapting in a positive manner to the obstacles presented while reducing the stress experienced and stress recovery. Problem–solving involves a person's ability to address adversity by identifying barriers and developing strategies to cope with those barriers. These factors help bring one back to a state of homeostasis or recovery.

The positive improvement(s) one experiences after a traumatic or series of traumatic events is referred to as posttraumatic growth and the experience itself is often considered to be of value in one's process of trauma recovery prompting a newly defined positive view of one's current and future life (Tedeschi and Calhoun, 2004; Sheikh, 2008; Vázquez, *et al.*, 2005).

With the protective factors of empathy, personality style, social supports, communication, and flexibility in new encounters at baseline, research has noted themes of posttraumatic growth for many individuals. These themes promote a forward thinking view of one's life in the areas of relationships, future opportunities, personal strength, and spiritual change (Tedeschi and Calhoun, 2004).

It is important to understand that while resilience and posttraumatic growth may appear similar, they are different. Resilience, discussed earlier, is the ability to bounce back to a familiar regime following a traumatic event, using one's cognitive abilities. However, not all resilient people experience posttraumatic growth. Posttraumatic growth is the ability to bring newer meaning of one's environment and a greater sense of appreciation for life's aspects that may have been overlooked prior to the trauma experience. According to Tedeschi and Calhoun (2004), people who experience posttraumatic growth often describe themselves as better than they were prior to the traumatic event.

There has been an increasing interest in a blended approach to direct practice when working with trauma victims. This blended approach would include information that comes from both epidemiological studies and nerve science, and efficacy studies on direct practice. For instance, practitioners may be able to draw from information obtained from neuroimaging that shows activity in the prefrontal cortex that helps them modify their treatment choice (Matto and Strolin-Goltzman, 2010). The material presented in this chapter was developed to inform practitioners of theoretical implications for practice when assisting individuals who have been exposed to trauma. Knowing how one's emotional development fosters lifelong success is valuable yet understanding the constructs that lead to those successes in the mist of trauma is of greater value.

Resilience, from a trauma-informed perspective is not a buzz word; it is a neuroscientific concept that reflects an individual's ability to return to a homeostatic state following a major stressor. Hope, coping, and hardiness lend to a positive cognitive triad that assist the person recovering from trauma and may foster resilience. Attachment theory, from a trauma-informed perspective, reflects how in early life development a bond with a nurturing adult provides a secure base for safety for a child and fosters exploration and the ability to create and sustain long-term relationships. As we will later discuss, disruption in attachment also can have lifelong consequences and interfere with recovery after trauma.

Chapter 5

Children and trauma

A growing body of research emphasizes the need for radical change on how we approach childhood trauma. In the first widespread global report on violence against children, Pinheiro (2006) reports legal or socially sanctioned forms of violence against children still exist, in some form, in all regions across the globe. The most extreme forms of violence occur against children occur in their homes, schools, or while under the care of others. According to Pinheiro's findings, an estimated 150 million girls and 73 million boys have been victims of some form of sexual violence; this form of violence most commonly occurs within the home by a perpetrator known to the child. Laws against corporal punishment protect only 2.4 percent of the total populations of the world's children. The World Health Organization cites the global impact of violence on children as a public health issue (World Health Organization, 2005). The recognition of the problem exists; the solution to the problem is more elusive.

In this chapter, we will explore the research findings related to the impact of trauma on the developing brain and offer a sample of treatment methods that can be adapted to fit within cultural norms and have demonstrated some hope for the future. The challenge of this task was that most of the research on efficacy comes out of Westernized countries. However, several models have been used in other parts of the world with good outcomes.

Children, more than any other population discussed in this book, experience the most changes in the microarchitecture of their brain as a result of experiencing trauma. Because of the advances in neuroimaging and neurochemical measurements, we may better understand the structural changes that occur within a developing brain when a child experiences trauma. These structural changes can contribute to learning difficulties, impulse control, and mood regulation. For these children, violence can literally change the structure of the brain which can result in dysfunction in fear extinction, cognitive reasoning, emotion regulation, and attachment. The intervention strategies offered later in this chapter attempt to provide evidence-supported options for helping children overcome the damage they may have experienced because of trauma, specifically related to symptoms related to fear extinction, cognitive reasoning, emotion regulation, and attachment.

Trauma, fear, and the developing brain

Chronic fear has a toxic effect on the developing brain of a child. In Chapter 3, we discussed the neurochemical response to fear and, if over utilized, the toxic after-effects it can have on the human body in general, and the brain in particular (Sapolsky, *et al.*, 2000; Mead, *et al.*, 2010). This toxic assault appears to be especially damaging to the developing brain of a child (Perry, 2009; Carrión, *et al.*, 2010; Twardosz and Lutzker, 2010). Children who are exposed to trauma via child abuse, witnessing violence, or experiencing a traumatic event are at higher risk of developing learning disorders, impulsivity problems, and mental disorders (Briere and Rickards, 2007; Perry, 2009; Carrión and Hull, 2010; Maheu, *et al.*, 2010). In this section we will focus on research findings within the neuroscience literature related to impact on trauma on the developing brain. In our review of the research, fear extinction, cognitive reasoning, emotion regulation, and attachment appear to cause the most distress for children who have experienced trauma, therefore we address these topics in our discussion of relevant neuroscience findings and include treatment methods that appear to offer consideration in these areas.

Human development continues across the lifespan; but the most industrious activity in brain development occurs in early childhood. While we now know that development of the prefrontal cortex and cognitive functioning continues into early adulthood (Sowell, *et al.*, 1999), many of the important structural connections that are essential to human well-being are already developed by the time we reach late adolescence. However, these structural connections can be interrupted by fear and threat, especially in a developing brain. The following sections describe the impact of fear on safety, emotion regulation, attentional and cognitive processing, and relationships.

Fear extinction and safety

Fear, as we generally understand it, can be physical and psychological. The function of the fear response, physically, has contributed to keeping the human species alive for millennia. However, over-activation of the fear response can cause long-term damage for all humans, but especially in children whose brains are still developing important structural connections (Perry, 2001; Anda, *et al.*, 2006). As we have already noted, the term *fear extinction* refers to the ability of the brain to return to a state of calm after a threat is no longer present. Learned fear responses continually trigger the stress system within the brain which reacts to traumatic cues as if the threat were still present (Carrión, *et al.*, 2010). This inability to return to a feeling a safety is also at the root of the diagnostic criterion for PTSD (American Psychiatric Association, 2000).

The hypothalamus, pituitary, and adrenal glands make up what is called the HPA axis and is the system called upon to coordinate the hormonal response to threat. Research in this field reveals this complex interplay of neurochemicals is connected to the fear response. While this neurochemical arsenal is essential to survival, chronic activation is not, and the negative effect of this assault appears to primarily target regulatory functions of the hippocampus, the amygdala, and the prefrontal cortex (Rodrigues, *et al.*, 2009).

The amygdala has a central role in interpreting information from the senses. Formation of emotional memories, particularly fear-related memories, also appear to be a function of the amygdala (LeDoux, 2000). It also has a central role in the fear circuitry within the brain: when activated, the amygdala bypasses the longer route, which involves the hippocampal and cortical regions, and goes directly to fight or flight. During times of what the amygdala considers threat, the ability of the hippocampus to place memories into context of space and time is suppressed. When this occurs, the memory remains in a "raw" state, and susceptible to triggers, or cues, that may be similar to the traumatic memory (Rogan, *et al.*, 1997; Sotres-Bayon, *et al.*, 2006). Therefore, activation of the fear-circuitry system in traumatized children does not remain isolated to past events. Experiences that do not elicit the fear responses in the brain are processed into long-term memory and stored within the cortical regions of the brain. This enables the experience to be put into context; we understand that the memory is of an event that happened in the past. When hippocampal function in processing memories is disrupted by major stressors (fear), this disruption may explain why traumatic experiences from the past are still vivid, although disjointed, in the present (Rodrigues, *et al.*, 2009). The prefrontal cortex, still in important formative stages during childhood, is the center for executive decision-making. Research shows that many adults who have experienced childhood trauma, have medial prefrontal cortex atrophy (Anda, *et al.*, 2006). There is evidence that the medial prefrontal cortex may, along with the amygdala and hippocampus, play an important role in fear extinction, and that damage within this system can contribute to the ongoing reactivation of the fear response experienced by trauma survivors (Sotres-Bayon, *et al.*, 2006; Grillon, 2008).

A major contributing factor to the brain's ability to carry out the function of fear extinction is predictability; the more predictable the environment, the safer a child feels. One consequence of not feeling safe is hypervigilance, or constant alertness to danger. This form of hyperarousal, once adaptive for safety, now can become a trait and can have lifelong consequences. Children who constantly feel threatened not only suffer physical and emotional damage, but often social isolation as well. In a study of 485 youth who were hospitalized in a child and youth psychiatric hospital, Azeem, *et al.* (2011) determined that high rates of youths being placed in seclusion or restraints had diagnoses of disruptive disorders and mood disorders. However, after implementing a trauma–informed care training program for the staff, the number of youth needing to be placed in restraints or seclusion dropped from 93 episodes to 31.

Emotion regulation and trauma

We have discussed the role of the hippocampus in cognitive reasoning; however, it appears to equally play an important role in emotion regulation as well. Hippocampal dysfunction has been linked to depression, bipolar disorder, and Cushing's disease (Brown, *et al.*, 1999; Rao, *et al.*, 2010). Learning to find a sense of safety and to be able to place traumatic memories in the context of their history may be compromised due to hippocampal abnormalities (Carrión, *et al.*, 2010).

Attentional bias and cognitive distortions

Any practitioner working with children should have a firm understanding of cognitive development. Understanding the impact trauma may have on children's memory, attention, learning, and language not only develops empathy, but enables a practitioner to choose an appropriate intervention for a child based on a proper assessment. A review of the literature (Hedges and Woon, 2001; Pechtel and Pizzagalli, 2011) on early life stress and the impact on cognitive development reveals a growing body of research that report dysfunction in the regions of the hippocampus, amygdala, and prefrontal cortex as a result of trauma or chronic stress. In children, the consequence of this dysfunction can be evidenced by learning difficulties, language development, attention deficits, and memory impairment. The effect of violence on the hippocampus, neuroendocrine system, and the prefrontal cortex has been a topic of continued interest to neuroscientists (Perry, 2001; Mead, *et al.*, 2010; Pechtel and Pizzagalli, 2011). Emotion regulation is dependent on pathways linking the paralimbic frontal cortex and the basal ganglia. The hippocampus is involved with the consolidation of explicit (declarative) memory from short- to long-term storage in the cortex (Campbell and MacQueen, 2004).

The hippocampus has an important role in both spatial and declarative memory. It is also critical for emotional processing and vulnerability to stress (Brown, *et al.*, 1999). There are numerous stress hormones within the body. Glucocorticoids have an important role in the functioning of metabolism, development, and a range of behaviors. Cortisol, which is a glucocorticoid, has been identified as the stress hormone that appears to be the most toxic to the hippocampus as a result of an over-activated fear circuitry (Perry, 2001; Mead, *et al.*, 2010; McEwen, 2013).

In a study by Carrión, *et al.* (2010) using fMRI, adolescents with and without PTSD symptoms were tested for memory function and behavioral symptoms. Their findings indicated abnormalities in the function of the hippocampus during memory processing among the adolescents with PTSD symptoms. Researchers hypothesize that cortisol secretions may also negatively affect the development of the prefrontal cortical region of the brain, resulting in difficulty with attention, memory, and regulation of emotion.

Relational challenges

Because a child's brain is dependent upon information from the outside environment to develop safety cues, trauma in early childhood can be especially disruptive in a child's ability to feel safe. As we have noted earlier, both neuroscience and Attachment Theory support the construct that safety is essential for well-being. If a child has not been able to form a secure attachment, their ability to feel safe is compromised. Deprivation of strong relationships can cause the brain to develop dysfunctional stress responses (Maheu, *et al.*, 2010; Twardosz and Lutzker, 2010). Caregiving is essential to child development. How a child experiences the caregiving experience affects neurobiological systems that control emotion regulation and stress responses (Perry, 2001; Cicchetti and Valentino, 2006). Studies on child maltreatment reveal that children who have been victims of neglect are also at risk of neurobiological dysfunction (Cicchetti and Lynch, 1995; Chugani, *et al.*, 2001; Cicchetti and Valentino, 2006).

Until recently, most of what we understood about the neurobiological impact of neglect came from animal studies. One of the first studies on the impact of childhood neglect on brain functioning came from a study of children in orphanages in Romania. In the 1980s, Romania experienced catastrophic economic turmoil, criminalization of the use of contraception, profound poverty, and government corruption. As a result, over 65,000 children were placed in orphanages; 85 percent of these children were not yet a year old. The majority of these children suffered neglect; many were victims of physical and sexual violence. In a study of ten children who had been adopted from Romania by US families, Chugani, *et al.* (2001) examined cognitive and behavioral deficits by utilizing positive emission tomography (PET). The children in the study had been placed in Romanian orphanages between the ages of four to six weeks and remained there for a mean of 38 months before they were adopted. At the time of the study, their ages ranged between 7–11 years. Malnutrition was indicated in nine of the ten children. Their adoptive parents reported developmental language delays in eight of the ten children. Additionally, the adoptive parents reported an absence of crying, toy play, sensory difficulties, and absence of using parents as an object of security. The result of the PET scans revealed dysfunctions in a number of limbic brain regions that may contribute to cognitive and behavioral deficits. There was evidence of dysfunction in the amygdala, the hippocampus, and bilaterally in the inferior temporal cortex (Chugani, *et al.*, 2001).

Uvnäs Moberg (2003), one of the foremost leaders worldwide in the field of oxytocin research, notes that physical contact, touching, in early life contributes to a child's ability to develop trusting relationships in the future. According to Uvnäs Moberg, the act of touching, and being touched, releases oxytocin. Oxytocin is both a hormone and a neurotransmitter. It is also part of the same system that produces fight or flight in times of stress. Uvnäs Moberg argues that 90 percent of research on the autonomic nervous system is focused on the sympathetic nervous system, the system activated in times of stress and defense. However, according to her research findings, there is more that needs to be understood about the *calm and connection* function of the autonomic nervous system (Uvnäs Moberg, 2003). From a trauma–informed treatment perspective, this appears to be sound advice. In the next section, we discuss some treatment modalities that assist children in working toward feeling calm and connected in the aftermath of their trauma experience.

Helping children recover from trauma

There is no universally accepted treatment method for trauma recovery. The treatment methods offered in the next section are supplied as examples of modalities that appear to have efficacy in treating children who have experienced trauma; many of them were developed with a trauma-focus. The National Child Traumatic Stress Network (NCTSN) and others have supported multiple trauma-informed modalities in the United States. Table 5.1 notes the commonalities between these models.

Duke, *et al.* (2010) reported that one in four youth in the US reported having experienced a traumatic event, which included a range from witnessing abuse of a parent to bullying and fighting. As research in trauma recovery considers the effects of trauma exposure on children and youth, the professional community also ponders the differences in the presentation of clinical symptoms of children as opposed to adults. The DSM-IV-TR (American Psychiatric Association, 2000) refers to several categories of symptoms that minimally meet the criteria for posttraumatic stress disorder. This disorder can be defined as witnessing, or experiencing, an event resulting in actual or perceived death or injury. Additionally, the symptoms experienced from this event range from recurring recollection of dreams and images of the event, persistent avoidance of stimuli associated with the event, and a heighted arousal state for at least one month (American Psychiatric Association, 2000). When considering the clinical symptoms of posttrauma exposure, children and youth present differently from adults. An adult may express intense fear, horror, or hopelessness. A child may present with agitation, disorganization, and insomnia. Where an adult may have repetitive thoughts that are disturbing, a child may display repetitive play that depicts aspects of the trauma experienced. Where an adult may relive the experience of the trauma with flashbacks or hallucinations, a child may re-enact the trauma itself (Carrión and Hull, 2010; American Psychiatric Association, 2000). Children and youth typically do not display the same patterns of behaviors as posttrauma adults, therefore it is becoming more established that the treatment interventions offered for adults would not benefit a child or youth. This chapter subsection will focus upon specific evidence-based treatment modalities developmentally appropriate for children and youth who have experienced trauma.

Table 5.1 Examples of trauma-informed treatment for children

	Treatment focus			
	Fear extinction	Emotion regulation	Attentional and cognitive strategies	Relational
Trauma Focused-CBT	Relaxation techniques, psychoeducation and narrative.	In vivo exposure to regulate emotions.	Cognitive coping techniques.	Parent–child sessions, ability to tell their story.
Cognitive and Cognitive Behavioral Therapy	Reduce symptoms associated with the trauma.	Acquire useful coping strategies.	Dispute negative thoughts with factual replacement.	Improved self-esteem and ability to relate with others.
CBT-Childhood Traumatic Grief	Stages of grief and loss. Narrative techniques.	Use of positive memories and coping strategies.	Narrative, letting go, moving on to safely, complete the grief process.	Parental involvement in sessions.
Play Therapy	Recreate symbolic replicas of people, places in a manner that reduces fear and ensures safety.	Play, drawing, creative arts to offset emotions that heighten anxiety and fear.	Art, storytelling, dance to restructure thinking into a more empowered manner.	Use of empathy to form trusting relationship with the practitioner.
Child–Parent Psychotherapy (CPP)	Free play with parent displaying the child's view of the trauma and reducing fear.	Restore appropriate affect while strengthening child parent relationship.	Restore child's sense of safety that results in improved cognition and behavior.	Use of social learning skills with parents to promote safe attachment.
Stanford Cue-Centered Therapy	Use of structured format for a sense of safety.	Narrative, relaxation, in vivo and imagery exposure ensuring safety.	Psychoeducation, cognitive restructuring associated with trauma cues.	Improved relations with peers and incorporates parent involvement and training.
Structured Psychotherapy for Adolescents Responding to Chronic Stress (SPARCS)	Used in schools and community settings where the child is already familiar and feels comfortable.	Use of techniques to manage mood and coping abilities.	Problem-solving and behavioral techniques to restructure cognition in a positive manner.	Group process allows for connections with peers in the group.
Skills Training in Affect and Interpersonal Regulation (STAIRS)	Group setting in familiar venue. Techniques to reduce fear of returning trauma.	Techniques to identify feelings while regulating emotional response.	Techniques that instill positive cognition to improve self-esteem and self-efficacy.	Gain skills in reducing conflicted relationships and fostering positive ones..

Source: adapted from the National Child Traumatic Stress Network.

Trauma Focused-Cognitive Behavioral Therapy

Trauma Focused–Cognitive Behavioral Therapy (TF–CBT) has become an important evidenced-based treatment modality for children and youth who have experienced a traumatic event(s) (Black, *et al.*, 2012; NICE, 2005). TF–CBT was created by Cohen, *et al.* (2006) after noting the efficacy of Sexual Abuse Specific-Cognitive Behavioral Therapy (SAS-CBT). While SAS-CBT was initially developed for children and youth exposed solely to sexual abuse, however, random clinical trials of participants exposed to additional types of trauma demonstrated its treatment efficacy for a larger population; it evolved into TF–CBT. It is utilized in practice with children ages 3–18 who have significant behavioral or emotional problems that are related to traumatic life events. It utilizes sessions with the child and parent/caregiver individually and jointly (NCTSN, n.d.).

TF–CBT is based on the following skills, best remembered by the acronym *PRACTICE*. They are:

- Psychoeducation and parenting skills
- Relaxation techniques
- Affective (mood) expression and regulation
- Cognitive coping
- Trauma narrative development and processing
- In vivo gradual exposure to trauma cues
- Conjoint parent/child sessions
- Enhancing safety.

(Cohen, *et al.*, 2012; Vickerman and Margolin, 2007.)

The basic framework of the TF–CBT model addresses traumatic cues that are supported by negative thoughts and reactionary behaviors (Vickerman and Margolin, 2007). Supporting a trauma-informed care approach, the initial phase of TF–CBT focuses upon building a trusting rapport with the client that includes a sense of safety. Coping strategies provide a child with the skill to substitute the ability to regulate a behavioral response to a traumatic cue. The psychoeducational phase identifies revolving themes resulting from the trauma that continue to repeat themselves throughout the youth experiences. The practitioner discusses the identified theme with the child so that the child can connect thoughts, feelings, and behaviors related to the trauma and how repeating these themes may impact his/her social relationships and self-identity (NCTSN, n.d.).

TF–CBT encourages a strengthened relationship between the child and the parent by fostering trust and support. It is important to provide skills for parents to promote their ability to separate, clearly in their minds, the incident of the trauma from their child. This is a key element in fostering a strong relationship between parent and child.

The initial phase of TF-CBT addresses the maladaptive ways a child/youth has coped with the stress endured from exposure to trauma. Affirmation of the child/youth's efforts to rebalance from the overwhelming effects of the trauma, even if the result were unfavorable, supports establishing trust. The practitioner then introduces coping strategies that may be effective without negative outcomes. The introduction of relaxation exercises occurs in this phase while paralleling the introduction of reminders of to be aware of "trauma cues" or situations that elicit a fear response. The child/youth, with time, is able to master the use of this strategy to move beyond the trauma cue in a successful risk-free manner that involves cognitive coping strategies and skill development in self-awareness (Cohen, et al., 2012; Vickerman and Margolin, 2007).

The core of the child/youth's environment generally rests with the home and family; therefore, involving the parents/caregiver of the child is essential. Ensuring that the parent comprehends the ramifications of the trauma on their child and the efforts they are making to move past the thoughts and behaviors associated with the trauma benefits all. Session(s) afforded to the child/youth and parent focus on:

- parental support;
- recognition of trauma cues and resultant negative behaviors; and
- understanding how the child/youth is using coping skills to offset the succession of affective dysregulation.

If the parent does not understand of the process of trauma, their inconsistent and often negative responses can further jeopardize the child's motivation to move beyond the trauma and they may continue to use maladaptive behaviors as a means to cope.

The second phase of TF-CBT builds upon the child/youth's ability to manage their emotions and awareness of the behaviors that are attributed to trauma memories. In this phase, the child/youth with the therapeutic support of the practitioner creates a narrative – a written document – about the themes that are associated with their trauma experience(s). As some children may be suffering from complex trauma, this skill may be more challenging to accomplish. It is the *process* of developing the narrative, rather than a completed narrative that is of therapeutic. The goal of the narrative process is for the child/youth to become better acquainted about their trauma experience and to be able to disconnect that association with their beliefs about themselves, their situation and their future.

While the child/youth is developing their narrative, the practitioner may be preparing their parent or guardian for the intensity of what they will hear from their child. The purpose of preparing the parent is to offset the possibility of any adverse reactions when presented with the complete narrative and to assess their ability to be fully involved in the recovery process for their child (Cohen, et al., 2012). The practitioner also remains focused on disputing negative beliefs and supporting any new, improved beliefs the child/youth may develop resulting from the narrative process. The practitioner also supports the child and parent to reinforce the new beliefs between them.

The final phase of TF-CBT is focused upon closure of the treatment process. In this phase, the plan is to shift trust from the practitioner to the parent. During this phase, the goal is education and training on safety and reminders on using new skills to manage future stressors and trauma reminders. As noted in earlier chapters, feeling safe is essential and the foundation for any intervention to work. Therefore, this phase of treatment reinforces new learned coping strategies and self-awareness while building future-focused methods managing future stressors.

Cognitive Behavioral Therapy

Cognitive Therapy (CT) and Cognitive Behavioral Therapy (CBT) have long been recognized as a formidable evidenced-based approach in assisting individuals with cognitive dysfunction manifest in psychological symptoms necessitating treatment (Ramchandani and Jones, 2003; Vickerman and Margolin, 2007; Black, et al., 2012; Makinson and Young, 2012). CBT, as we understand it today, is a merging of behavioral theory and cognitive theory, largely based on the work of Aaron Beck. According to the Beck Institute (Beck Institute, n.d.), CT has been demonstrated efficacy in over 1,000 studies for depression, anxiety disorders, addictions, and eating disorders.

In terms of development, CBT is not a trauma-informed approach; meaning that it was not developed to specifically address the symptoms that we have been discussing throughout this book. However, it has been used for treating trauma survivors and is the foundation for most of the trauma-informed modalities offered for review in this text. The intent of CBT is to identify and change thoughts that contribute to feelings and behaviors that have a negative connection to the trauma experience. Employing strategies of cognitive restructuring and behavioral changes, the goal is to offset the triggers of the traumatic memories, thus reducing, if not eliminating, the negative response and feeling (Vickerman and Margolin, 2007).

CBT is routinely used with adults, and is being used more often with children who have experienced trauma such as sexual abuse and natural disasters (Cohen and Mannarino, 1998; Deblinger, et al., 1999; Scheeringa, et al., 2007). Following the terrorists attacks in New York City on September 11, 2001, there were substantial efforts to provide treatment services to children and youth by the Child and Adolescent Trauma Treatment Services Project (CATS). CATS identified children and youth with mild to severe symptoms of posttraumatic stress disorder. Those with mild symptoms were provided with a four-session regime of CBT treatment; those youth with greater severity of symptoms were provided sessions utilizing TF-CBT. The outcome measure of this study revealed a reduction of symptoms for both groups (CBT and TF-CBT), however those who received TF-CBT demonstrated greater improvement. Of significance is that the improvement for all youth was sustained when re-measured six months post-treatment (CATS Consortium, 2007, 2010). This approach is consistent with the recommendation that TF-CBT be used with children whose symptoms are more severe and are interfering with their ability to function (NCTSN, n.d.).

Scheeringa, et al. (2007) conducted research with children under the age of five years soon after their exposure to individual traumatic events (auto accident, Hurricane Katrina). Utilizing a 12-session format that was based on CBT theory, and the Parent–Child Weekly Rating Scale (PCWRS), both studies noted a significant reduction in PTSD symptoms when parents were involved in all treatment session (Scheeringa, et al., 2007).

Trauma-Focused Childhood Traumatic Grief

The model of Trauma-Focused Childhood Traumatic Grief (TF-CTG) is based upon the TF-CBT model for treatment of children and youth who have been exposed to trauma. Emergent research depicts the child or youth who is exposed, either directly or indirectly, to violence may develop a disorder call Childhood Trauma Grief. This term refers to when a child or youth symptoms from trauma exposure prevent them from grieving from the trauma in a manner that will allow them to regain their balance and complete the bereavement process (Cohen, et al., 2006; Crenshaw, 2006).

This modality goes beyond TF-CBT to specify a greater focus on children and youth exposed to trauma, but have been unable to complete the bereavement process due to their overwhelming symptoms. These symptoms are the result of any memory, or reminder, of the trauma and loss that results in the child being re-traumatized (Cohen and Mannarino, 2004; Crenshaw, 2006). The authors further posit that it is of importance for the child's recovery to include grief-focused treatment in addition to trauma-focused treatment. When the trauma-focused treatment also includes elements to address the trauma, loss, and bereavement at minimum, it has been shown there is a reduction in child's traumatic grief symptoms (Layne, et al., 2001).

The Cognitive Behavioral Therapy for Childhood Traumatic Grief is a 15-week manualized modality and is administered to children individually with parental involvement in some of the sessions. The sessions include psychoeducation that promotes: an acknowledgment of feelings and mood associated with loss, relaxation techniques, the cognitive connection of thoughts, feelings and behaviors; coping skills, writing and sharing a narrative of the trauma with one's parent; stages of grief and loss and the unresolved issues that remain; focus upon positive memories and being able to permit oneself to grieve fully (Cohen, et al., 2004). Crenshaw (2006) recommends utilizing a prescriptive model that is aligned closer to Attachment Theory. Within this perspective, there is a focus upon 12 areas that are included in the cognitive treatment approach: the creation of a sense of safety with the practitioner modeling attachment; the reality of one's loss; the expression of grief; formal ways to remember the loss; addressing ambivalence; resolving the ambivalence; preserving the memories; timeless attachment; writing about one's connections; letting go; moving on; and termination from therapy. Utilizing this variation of TF-CTG found that placing greater emphasis on safety within the therapeutic relationship provides the likelihood the child will be able to complete the process of grief and reduce those symptoms and behaviors, while fostering new memories and rituals of remembering their loss.

Play therapy

Children's play is an expression of their developing thought process while modeling adults and their roles and those of others in the child's world (Erikson, 1963). Play is a child's work and a means by which they learn not only about their skills and aptitudes but also about how to socially engage in their environment. The modality of play therapy has been used by many child practitioners within a myriad of situations, including with those children who have been exposed to trauma and violence. In this modality, a child can communicate and gain an understanding of their feelings resulting from traumatic events by use of drawings, play, and other artistic and expressive mediums. Children who have been exposed to trauma seek the protection of their parents from further trauma. But if that parent is unavailable to provide safety due to mental illness, incarceration, substance abuse, or location, the child can may feel abandoned and plunge into an abyss of isolation and disengage from others. They may attempt to protect themselves from further harm by anger toward self and others. As a result, they may be poor in academic studies and experience punishment as a result of this behavior.

The use of empathy in play therapy provides a safe forum to build a trusting and therapeutic relationship between child and practitioner (Crenshaw and Hardy, 2007). For children and youth with complex trauma, this process is often challenging and may be unsuccessful unless the practitioner's use of empathy remains present. The use of a play therapy method allows the child to gain a better understanding of the trauma that occurred and the effects it has had on them, while mastering their emotions and gaining acknowledgment of their feelings about their experience (Van Fleet, et al., 1999). The use of a sand tray is common in play therapy and allows the child to create their narrative about what they are experiencing. To be able to play in a sandbox and create symbolic replicas of people, places, and/or natural elements (i.e. weather) provides a natural platform for the child's language of play and provides the practitioner insight into the child's perspective (Van Fleet, et al., 1999).

Play therapy as a treatment approach has been gaining validity for use with children who have suffered sexual abuse (Bratton, et al., 2005; Harvey, 2008; Reyes and Asbrand, 2005). A meta-analysis of 93 play therapy studies revealed that children who received play therapy functioned better than the children who received no treatment. Non-directive play therapy produced greater treatment results than directive play therapy approaches for reducing behavior problems (Bratton, et al., 2005).

In a study conducted by Reyes and Asbrand (2005), children treated for sexual abuse were assessed initially and then again, nine months into treatment using the Trauma Checklist for Children. At the nine-month measure, the outcomes revealed a decrease in symptoms of anxiety, posttraumatic stress, and depression, to a non-clinical level (Reyes and Asbrand, 2005). While not all symptoms were fully eradicated, these findings on symptom reduction are encouraging.

In a modified approach to play therapy and closely associated with family therapy, Harvey (2008) developed Dynamic Play Therapy. Within this model, all family members are engaged in sessions. The sessions involve acting, arts, movement, and storytelling (Harvey, 1993, 2008). Within the Dynamic Play model, the child is able to play and describe the trauma, and their feelings, while their parent/caregivers are guided by the practitioner on how to provide support to the child. Parent/caregivers and children collaborated their play actions in order to improve their cohesion during a difficult time while recovering from a trauma.

Harvey (2008) conducted a study of families with children presenting with high risk symptomology, such as suicidal thoughts and self-harming behaviors, as a result of having been exposed to interpersonal trauma. These children and their families received Dynamic Play Therapy over an 18-month period. The parent/caregivers rated their child's presenting symptoms using the Child Behavior Checklist at the beginning and at the end of treatment. The results reflected lower ratings of the serious presenting problems at the end of treatment.

Child–Parent Psychotherapy (CPP)

Child–Parent Psychotherapy (CCP) began in the mid-1980s at the Child Trauma Research Program at the University of California, San Francisco Department of Psychiatry. In the US, CCP is listed by the NCTSN as an evidence-based approach to treating children who have been exposed to trauma (NREPP, n.d.). The CPP model is designed for treatment of children, ages five and up, who have been exposed to trauma and includes components of psychodynamic, cognitive behavioral, and attachment theories. The modality incorporates social learning skills while intervening and supporting a child's ability to attach to their parent, even if the parent may have emotional limitations. Strengthening this bond has demonstrated to be beneficial to both the child and the parent (Lieberman, et al., 1997, 2005, 2006).

CPP is a manualized treatment modality that focuses on supporting the child's safe response to danger while enhancing a strong attachment relationship with their parent (NREPP, n.d.). The format is lengthy for the child and parent/caregiver (50 weekly sessions). Free play is utilized to display the child's view of the violence witnessed and to encourage and foster social interaction with their parent/caregiver (Lieberman, et al., 2005). In addition to the joint child–parent play sessions, the parent receives individual therapy to foster understanding of age-appropriate behaviors of their child. Lieberman, et al. (2005) identify the following focus and corresponding strategies for CPP:

- domains of functioning of play
- sensorimotor disorganization and disruption of biological rhythms
- fearfulness
- recklessness
- self-endangering and accident prone behavior
- aggression
- punitive and critical parenting
- the relationship to the perpetrator of the violence.

Research studies on the efficacy of CPP have demonstrated applicability of this model across cultures. Many of the studies have been with children who have been traumatized by domestic violence (Lieberman, *et al.*, 2006; NREPP, n.d.).

Group treatment with child survivors of trauma

While many practitioners may prefer to provide individual treatment for children and adolescents who have been exposed to trauma, it is not always feasible, or efficacious, to do so. Accessibility to treatment centers may be limited and individual treatment is very expensive. Group sessions can provide treatment in an arena where natural groups exists, such as schools, neighborhood associations, and centers of worship. Many groups for children and youth occur in school settings where the group process can be monitored and evaluated. Group treatment is often based upon the Cognitive Behavioral Therapy model with a structured format. Some group formats are described here.

An example of trauma-informed group treatment is the Stanford cue-centered therapy (SCCT) model. SCCT was developed at the Stanford Early Life Stress Research program within the Department of Psychiatry at the School of Medicine at Stanford University, CA. This structured manualized treatment is designed to treat children who have experienced trauma. SCCT brings techniques from other evidenced-based modalities that are specific to a child's developmental stage (Carrion and Hull, 2010).

This model of treatment was developed as a trauma-informed model that recognizes that trauma can cause maladaptive cognitive, emotional, physiological, and behavioral symptoms. SCCT is similar to the multimodal of Arnold Lazarus (1989). Within this model, there is a focus on "trauma cues" that spark negative reactions when triggered (Carrión and Hull, 2010). The approach presents recovery techniques to the group in the following ways:

- psychoeducation
- relaxation
- narrative
- in vivo and imagery exposure
- parental involvement and training.

The intent of these foci is to empower the youth and their parents with new insights to the trauma cues that will prompt the maladaptive behaviors and can lead to interference in school functioning, social relationships, and health. As described by Carrión and Hull (2010), SCCT is implemented over 15-week sessions. The materials are presented in a systematic order allowing for a progression of skill acquisition related to self-awareness, knowledge, and tools to use beyond the completion of the treatment series. In the first phase, generally three sessions, the youth and parent/caregiver are taught emotion-regulation relaxation techniques and provided education about the SCCT program. They also work to develop skills that can be utilized when threatened with a traumatic cue or trigger. During the second phase of four sessions, the youth learns narrative techniques, and retells the story of his/her trauma. During this retelling, the practitioner offers empathy and safety designed to strengthen cognitive processing rather than reactive cues. In the final or third phase, the practitioner continues to reinforce positive cognitive restructuring of the youths' negative cognitions related to their trauma experience by utilizing the skills learned in the previous sessions. Research on the efficacy of this group treatment model have been promising (Black, *et al.*, 2012; Carrión and Hull, 2010). Findings reflect a decrease in the presenting symptoms at completion of the 15-week session. Currently, this modality is being utilized in schools in California with plans to further validate the model's efficacy with additional research.

SPARCS: Structured psychotherapy for adolescents responding to chronic stress

SPARCS is also a manualized treatment program for children and adolescents exposed to trauma. SPARCS is a 16-week group treatment program than is often offered in schools and community agencies. This CBT-designed program includes components of mindfulness, dialectical behavior therapy, problem-solving, and social supports. The focus is on acquiring skills to manage mood and behavior that may have been problematic as a result of trauma (DeRosa and Pelcovitz, 2006; Weiner, *et al.*, 2009). Goals of SPARCS include developing coping strategies, to cultivate consciousness, and to create connections with others. The model demonstrates efficacy in decreased trauma-related symptomology, especially for African-American youth.

STAIR: Skills training in affect and interpersonal regulation

Developed by the Institute of Trauma and Stress at NYU Child Study Center, this CBT model focuses on core components of complex trauma intervention (Silva, *et al.*, 2003; Cook, *et al.*, 2005). The STAIR model was developed primarily for treatment of adolescent girls, ages 12–21, who have experienced any range of trauma, from sexual abuse, physical abuse, or community violence. The goals of the treatment are:

- identification and labeling of feelings
- the development of emotion regulation skills
- practice with handling distress-inducing interpersonal situations
- development of self-esteem/self-efficacy.

This model is conducted in a series of 10–15 weekly sessions that can be individual or group. The sessions focus upon skill-building regarding emotion regulation and social relationships. There is a component of imagery with a narrative retelling in the later individual session portion of the model so as to reduce re-traumatization for the child or adolescent (Silva, *et al.*, 2003). Research findings indicate that when used with adolescent girls, there was a reduction of symptoms for depression, PTSD, and dissociation and an improvement in emotion regulation; however, school performance did not change after treatment.

Hope for the future

Many of the treatment methods provided in this chapter include strengthening social support (parent or interpersonal) and not simply and individual focus. In a study of 210 immigrant and local youths in Hong Kong, Wong (2008) found that peer relations appeared to serve as a supportive factor in promoting coping skills and well-being. Parental conflicts were noted to be a major source of stress for these youths; however, peer support appeared to mitigate the impact of the conflict.

There is great importance in advocating for community involvement in restoring safety for children who have been physically or sexually abused. Noting that a child's environment needs to be safe to continue their recovery from trauma, the inclusion of school, street, and neighborhood safety is of importance. The inclusion of community organizations to work toward this end is the means to increase the safety net for children at risk (Van Fleet, *et al.*, 1999; Carrión and Hull, 2010). As we move forward in treatment from a trauma-informed perspective, some methods may fall by the wayside because they do not target the important areas need for children to recovery from trauma.

Chapter 6

Adult survivors of childhood trauma

As we explored in Chapter 4, structural changes can occur within a developing brain of a child when exposed to prolonged periods of fear. What then happens, when that same child enters into adulthood? Do those structural changes continue to impact fear extinction, cognitive reasoning, emotion regulation, attachment, and relationships? According to an extensive body of research, the answer, sadly, appears to be "yes." In this chapter, we will expand our discussion to include the challenges adult survivors of childhood trauma experience. In many ways, the research in this area is more profound than the studies on children; the dataset is larger and much harder to ignore. As we have already noted, prolonged exposure to elevated cortisol levels triggered by the stress response in the brain, can contribute to damage of the hippocampus and the prefrontal cortex, contributing to deregulation in fear extinction, disruption in memory processing, depression, anxiety, impulsivity, difficulty in developing trust, and the ability to sustain relationships. Hippocampal atrophy has been reported in adult survivors of childhood trauma diagnosed with PTSD (Bremner, 2007). Additionally, altered functioning of the prefrontal cortex (Bremner, *et al.*, 1999) and elevated cortisol reactivity to stress (Heim and Nemeroff, 2001) has been reported in studies of adult survivors of childhood trauma. Therefore, it is not surprising to find correlations in the literature between childhood trauma and the following symptoms in adults:

- alcohol and drug misuse and addiction
- depression
- anxiety
- mood regulation
- relational issues
- chronic, life-limiting medical conditions.

(Anda, *et al.*, 2006; Dhabhar, *et al.*, 2012.)

The symptoms noted above go beyond those identified by a diagnosis of PTSD. They are more complex and can be traced to when neurocognitive development is most vulnerable – childhood. Because of this complexity, van der Kolk, *et al.* (2005) proposed a new diagnostic category called Developmental Trauma Disorder which better captures the complexity symptom presentation as a result of cumulative trauma. A large study in Japan of 2,959 men and 279 women (Izutsu, *et al.*, 2004), examined the impact of past traumatic events on stress tolerance, anxiety, and depression. After assessing for past trauma experiences, the subjects were divided into two groups; those who were "trauma-exposed" and those who were "non-exposed." The findings revealed that the males in the trauma-exposed group had significantly higher rates of depression, anxiety, and job stress than the males in the non-exposed group. Females in the trauma-exposed group had significantly higher rates of anxiety than the non-exposed group.

While there is significant research on symptomatology found in adult survivors of adult trauma (Izutsu, *et al.*, 2004; Anda, *et al.*, 2006; Walsh, *et al.*, 2007; Cloitre, *et al.*, 2009; Felitti and Anda, 2009), one of the most imposing endeavors that captures the nature of complex trauma is the Adverse Childhood Experiences (ACE) Study in the United States. The study is collaboration between the US Centers for Disease Control and Prevention (CDC) and Kaiser Permanente's Department of Preventative Medicine. With more than 9 million members, Kaiser Permanente is one of the largest not-for-profit health insurance plans in the United States (Kaiser Permanente, n.d.). The largest of its kind, this longitudinal study of over 17,000 subjects has collected data on traumatic experiences during the first 18 years of life. It is important to note that the participants were voluntary, middle-class residents from San Diego, California, insured by Kaiser Permanente, had access to medical care, and ethnically representative of the US overall. There were nearly an equal number of males and females in the study. The sample provides a "snap-shot" of most populations in the US and makes the findings harder to dispute.

Participants in the ACE study were asked to respond to eight categories of adverse *childhood experiences* in the initial implementation of the study; two scores on neglect were added during the second implementation for a total of ten. They were clustered under abuse, household dysfunction, and neglect (Felitti and Anda, 2009) and are as follows:

- Abuse
    - emotional (threats and humiliation)
    - physical (beating, not spanking)
    - contact sexual abuse

- Household dysfunction
  - ○ mother was treated violently
  - ○ household member was an alcoholic or drug user
  - ○ household member was imprisoned
  - ○ household member was chronically depressed, suicidal, mentally ill, or in a psychiatric hospital
  - ○ not raised by both biological parents
- Neglect
  - ○ physical
  - ○ emotional.

(Adverse Childhood Experiences Study, n.d.; Felitti and Anda, 2009.)

Upon the participant's completion of the questionnaire, an ACE score was determined for that individual. The ACE score is a count of the number of *categories* of experiences, not individual instances, which occurred in the participant's childhood and adolescent years. The ACE scores were then matched with the participants' current state of well-being, then tracked through emergency room visits, doctor's appointments, hospitalizations, prescriptions, and finally death.

The initial findings from the ACE study revealed that of the 17,000 participants, only one-third had an ACE score of 0 (no adverse childhood experiences). Their findings revealed that the higher number of categories (ACE score) experienced, the higher the association between depression, use of antidepressant prescriptions, and suicide attempts. Additional findings indicated that there were also strong associations between higher ACE scores and smoking, alcoholism, intravenous drug use, and poor job performance. Finally, higher ACE scores were connected with liver disease, chronic obstructive pulmonary disease (COPD), coronary artery disease (CAD), and autoimmune disease. These findings are congruent with other smaller studies and give solid credence to a trauma-informed approach not only by mental health and social care agencies but by the medical community as well (Felitti and Anda, 2009).

Fear extinction in adults

The emerging research related to dysfunction in fear extinction reveals that adult survivors of childhood trauma may experience distress in numerous areas of their lives (Izutsu, *et al.*, 2004; van der Kolk, *et al.*, 2005; Walsh, *et al.*, 2007; Cloitre, *et al.*, 2009). The function of the stress/fear circuitry within the brain and the ability to return to *basal* (homeostatic) functioning is a subject relevant to any practitioner who works with trauma survivors.

Treatment is irrelevant if it solely targets higher-level cognitive functions. These functions are simply not accessible if the stress/fear circuitry of the brain is overactive; safety trumps everything within the brain (Sapolsky, 2004; LeDoux, 2012; McEwen, *et al.*, 2012). Because fear extinction should be a primary goal of any trauma-informed approach to working with adult survivors of childhood trauma, a general knowledge of this circuitry is essential to understanding why some methods of treatment may work, and others are ineffective and potentially harmful.

Emotion regulation

Neuroscience research on emotion regulation provides insight into our understanding of the impact of cumulative trauma on the ability to regulate emotion. Studies on emotion regulation reveal during *reappraisal strategies* there is decreased activation in the amygdala and increased activity in the prefrontal cortex (Kim, *et al.*, 2011). Reappraisal is an internal cognitive-linguistic process that down-regulates emotional experiences. Frequent use of reappraisal, over time, leads to enhanced emotion regulation. Conversely, *suppression* results in decreased expressive behavior and increased activity in the sympathetic nervous system (Goldin, *et al.*, 2009). Neuroimaging of these two processes reveal that reappraisal strategies resulted in enhanced signals in the medial, dorsolateral and ventrolateral regions of the prefrontal cortex and decreased activity in the amygdala (Goldin, *et al.*, 2009).

The ability to self-regulate stress responses such as anxiety, anger, and aggressive behavior may be a neurobiological result of chronic exposure to trauma (Cloitre, *et al.*, 2009). The number of traumas experienced before the age of 18 is associated with a larger degree of symptom complexity (Briere, *et al.*, 2008). Dysfunction in the fear circuitry of the brain as a result of over-activation can cause both avoidant behavior and over-stimulated behavior when confronted with trauma cues.

Attentional bias and cognitive distortions

Adults who have experienced childhood trauma may struggle with attentional bias and cognitive reasoning. Attentional bias refers to hyperarousal to cues or triggers in the environment that are reminders of threat. This hyperarousal can interfere with the ability to focus on current events and interfere with social functioning. The function of the prefrontal cortex promotes decision making, abstract thinking and regulating mood (Dias, *et al.*, 1996). As noted above, hyperarousal in the fear circuitry causes dysfunction in the prefrontal cortex, contributes to attentional bias, and inhibits cognitive reasoning.

Reason is not part of the survival system of the brain. According to what we understand of evolutionary biology, the complex nature of the cortex is the one thing that sets humans apart from other mammals. The development of the structural circuitry of the cortex, that enables adults to "think things through," can be altered by trauma in childhood. The clinical implications for this knowledge are profound. Treatment that solely relies on cognitive restructuring ignores fundamental neurobiology. However, as we discuss further in this chapter, many treatment methods include cognitive restructuring as a fundamental construct. Fortunately, many have adapted to include strategies for safety in their initial phases.

When we sense threat, our internal state shifts; we become vigilant. In a vigilant state, there is an increase in the sympathetic nervous system activity that causes increased heart rate, blood pressure, breathing, and a release of glucose to prepare us to fight or flee. In a state of hypervigilance, the brain blocks out all non-essential critical information. The effect on prefrontal connectivity is an adaptive feature in the short run; thinking too much can get you killed when faced with immediate threat. However, over-activation of this system appears to carry-over in humans and continues to blunt prefrontal connectivity (Koenen, *et al.*, 2001; Liston, *et al.*, 2009). Evidence suggests that because of over-activation of this system in childhood, adult survivors of childhood trauma often struggle with anxiety, cognitive processing (Perry, 2001; Mead, *et al.*, 2010), and learning-related difficulties (Anda, *et al.*, 2006; Liston, *et al.*, 2009).

As a result of the cognitive challenges adult survivors of childhood trauma may experience, they may have difficulty starting new tasks, generating alternative solutions in problem-solving, feel easily overwhelmed, and struggle maintaining self-esteem (Hedges and Woon, 2011). Each of these symptoms can be a challenge in treatment. In order to learn new things, the brain must be in a state of calm. Creativity and problem-solving are not functions of the brain in an anxious state (Perry, 2006). According to neuroscience, in order to be able to develop cognitive reasoning skills, a person must reach a state of calm (Perry, 2006; Kim, *et al.*, 2011).

Relationships and adult survivors of childhood trauma

Humans are social creatures. According to Uvnäs Moberg (2003), the hypothalamus and pituitary are two important brain regions that play a large role in establishing human connection, the release of oxytocin. In animal studies, oxytocin has been associated with social contact, maternal behavior, less anxiety, sleep-inducement and a state of calm, and facilitated learning. In humans, oxytocin levels increase during breastfeeding and are considered to help both infant and child create a bond (attachment). This bond becomes the foundation for the perception of safety and may have lifelong implications. Adverse childhood experiences can disrupt the ability to form essential attachments.

Oxytocin is important for regulatory functions and moderating stress. It lowers blood pressure and pulse rate and mitigates the flooding of stress hormones into the blood stream (Uvnäs Moberg, 2003). Adult survivors of childhood trauma who do not form secure attachments may produce less oxytocin during time of stress then adults without a trauma history (Pierrehumbert, et al., 2012). As we have already noted, adult survivors of childhood trauma may have a sensitized stress circuitry that makes it difficult to distinguish the quality of relationships. Insecure attachment in women with PTSD has been associated with low self-esteem, feared loss of attachment figures, and perceived lack of social support (Stalker, et al., 2005). There is a high association between persons diagnosed with Borderline Personality Disorder (BPD) and childhood trauma (Sadock and Sadock, 2007). That features of BPD are evidenced by impulsivity, mood instability, low self-esteem, and difficulty sustaining relationships. There is evidence that indicate that many persons with BPD have smaller hippocampal and amygdala volumes than those without BPD (Schmahl, et al., 2009).

Adult survivors of childhood trauma face challenges that go beyond the psychological aspect of recovery from trauma; they must, quite literally, re-train their brain. The burgeoning research emerging related to this population leave little doubt of the neurobiological impact of cumulative trauma. In the following section, we provide a sampling of some of the most researched treatment methods for this population. From a trauma-informed perspective, treatment should attend to promoting fear extinction and calm, cognitive reasoning, emotion regulation, and building relationships.

Treatment for adult survivors of childhood trauma

In the helping professions, assisting individuals to return to a state of individual success and independence posttrauma involves a key component; the establishment of a therapeutic relationship utilizing a trauma-informed approach. Using a trauma-informed approach allows for client engagement, and the establishment of trust and mutual respect between the practitioner and the individual who has experienced the trauma. This is of even greater importance for adults who have experienced childhood trauma. These individuals often experience the inability to regulate emotions which can then lead to psychopathology in adult life (Anderson and Alexander, 1996; Roche, et al., 1999; Muller, et al., 2000). In cases of sexual, physical, or emotional abuse, witnessing ongoing domestic violence, or removal from one's home to another, the effects of such traumatic experiences can have an untoward influence upon the child-now-adult's ability to establish successful relationships. Thus the therapeutic relationship is a step in changing the cycle of limited, or no, success in establishing relationships for adult survivors of childhood trauma.

Cognitive Behavioral Therapy (CBT)

Cognitive Behavioral Therapy (CBT) is directed toward disputing one's negative thinking. This advances a cognitive shift from negative to positive thinking, emotions, and behaviors and often leads to reduced emotional and behavioral symptoms. CBT has been effecting in improving daily performance in social, occupational, and spiritual realms. The skill applied by the trained practitioner in challenging the client's fortified negative schema is at the core of this modality. It seeks to promote the strengths of the person who has been anchored in a negative cognitive triad; they are not good, their situation is not good, and therefore their future is bleak (Beck, 1991, 2008).

Makinson and Young (2012) note that there is supporting evidence of the biological connection between the prefrontal cortex of the brain and thought activation when CBT is utilized. The prefrontal cortex manages the ability to think and regulate emotion. When a client is presented with techniques that challenge, or dispute, negative thoughts, the prefrontal cortex demonstrates activity. Negative thoughts, especially in adult survivors of childhood trauma, signal threat. Along with the amygdala, the prefrontal cortex is challenged with determining if the threat is real or not. The cumulative effect of trauma can interfere with this process and the prefrontal cortex function can be diminished. The amygdala function, designed to react to threat, prompts an emotional (stress) response without the cognitive, rational, assistance of the prefrontal cortex (LeDoux, 2000; Banks, et al., 2007). Thus, it does not matter if a negative thought is based upon a current reality or past traumatic event; the amygdala sends signals to respond to the thought (stressor), typically a negative emotional reaction. Though originally conceptualized for treating depression (Beck, 1991), research on CBT demonstrates positive results that are long-lasting when applied to adult survivors of childhood trauma. Success in "rewiring" the brain to moderate the emotional response to a trauma trigger requires the client to consistently challenge maladaptive thinking patterns and create new, constructive views of themselves, their world, and their future.

STAIR

Skills Training in Affective and Interpersonal Regulation (STAIR) is a CBT approach that addresses one's ability to regulate emotion (Cloitre, *et al.*, 2002). When affect (mood) deregulation occurs, a person has limited stress tolerance and an intensive emotional reaction to stimuli, and is often unable to settle and compose him- or herself. With the STAIR approach, the goal is to assist with emotion regulation and to improved social relationships.

In a study by Cloitre, *et al.* (2002), 200 women over the age of 18 years who met the criteria for PTSD related to childhood abuse were provided 16 sessions of STAIR. The control group of women also meeting the criteria for PTSD was wait-listed for treatment. Treatment areas addressed in this model include:

- the identification of feelings
- emotional management
- distress tolerance
- acceptance of feelings
- identifying trauma–based schemas
- identification of conflict between the feelings and personal goals
- issues of power and control
- role play to assist in developing interpersonal relationships with a balance of power.

This study added a second phase of treatment utilizing Prolonged Exposure therapy (discussed in greater detail in Chapter 8) using a modification of imagery exposure to the traumatic event(s) followed by coping strategies when faced with life stressors. According to the study findings, with this combined approach, there was improvement in the areas of emotional regulation and interpersonal skills, and reduction in PTSD symptoms (Cloitre, *et al.*, 2002).

Creative therapies

Creative therapies allow for self-expression through mediums of arts, dance, drama, poetry, play therapy, and other forms of artistic expression (Malchiodi, 2011). In trauma recovery, this approach is therapeutic when it fosters the formation of a therapeutic alliance and trust. The current use of this modality promotes music, play, drama, and music to promote emotion regulation and fear extinction in adult survivors of childhood trauma.

Meekums (1999) researched the effectiveness of a three-phase creative therapy approach to trauma recovery with adult survivors of childhood sexual abuse. This study determined that creating a therapeutic alliance allowed for the survivor to tell their story of survival and "let go" of memories and grief through the use of creative methods. The involvement of creative therapy allows for the memory of the traumatic event to recede into the past becoming less intrusive in one's daily life.

Malchiodi (2011) promotes the integration of *mindful* practices in a trauma-informed approach, while enhancing resilience utilizing expressive arts therapy. This would include the following five components:

1   Stabilize the body's response using a "neurosequential approach" via expressive arts therapies.
2   Use a trauma-informed evaluation and sensory-based activities using expressive arts to identify the body's reactions to stressful events and memories.
3   Utilize somatic and sensory approaches to self-regulation to respond to the body's reactions to traumatic events.
4   Use reconnection with positive attachment and self-soothing to reinforce a sense of safety.
5   Normalize and enhance resilience, and build strengths by using the arts.

Narrative Therapy

Narrative Therapy is an evidence-based approach that allows for adult survivors of childhood trauma to understand the meaning of a memory or experience, and not as a cause for an undesired emotion or behavior. A behavior associated with any experience may be dictated by that experience. The goal of Narrative Therapy is for the person to know more of their experience by assigning meaning to the experience, gain insight that the experience was something that occurred *to* them, and then promoting distance from a negative behavioral response related to that experience.

When the perception of a person's "story" directs their behavior in a maladaptive way, the role of the therapist is to assist the client in deconstructing their unproductive stories and reconstruct new ones that are more productive. The goal of this process is to create a new and more optimistic account of that experience (Nichols, 2013). The process of the client recreating their past story in way manner that is less destructive to their well-being also promotes personal growth and self-efficacy (Courtois, et al., 2009).

Plummer and Knudson-Martin (1996) found that the use of Narrative Therapy generally allows users to create a story of how they would have acted differently, in a proactive manner, in their social experiences. The new story further allows them to be actively engaged in their current and future social experiences, rather than reliving the past. Utilizing a hermeneutics approach (interpreting language in a philosophical manner), the research focused upon the images of the clients' stressors and how their behavior was affected by the images. The subjects for this study were ten volunteers who met a criterion for "at risk youth" when they were younger, but were now adults. The findings indicated that the adults who appeared to be resilient retold their story with the use of images of strength and understanding, which appeared to furthered impression of having "escaped" or survived their past situation. For those whose memories of negative images were strongest, the use of the hermeneutic processing approach helped them depict positive cues that fostered the therapeutic relationship and verbal narrative. In both responses, the use of the narrative approach was a pivotal point in the therapeutic process toward the goal of seeing oneself separate from the stressful event.

In a larger study, Leahy, et al. (2003) compared groups of volunteers with a history of childhood sexual abuse. The volunteers' current symptom presentation was evaluated utilizing the Trauma Symptom Inventory, which then determined whether they were clinically or non-clinically impaired by the stress from their childhood sexual abuse history. Their use of a trauma narrative provided for greater recall of the traumatic event(s) resulting in greater description of affective detail and understanding. For example, those who rated as clinically distressed noted that, at the time, they were unable to regulate feelings such as fear and now as adults reported continued anger, grief and difficulty with establishing relationships. Those who did not rate as clinically distressed, reported feeling shame and shock at that time but currently reported anger or no affective influence. The benefit of this modality for those who are adult survivors of childhood trauma is the opportunity to gain an understanding, and ascribe a meaning to those past events that, in their current life, provides them with the new-found understanding of their ability to survive. They learn how to separate themselves from their past trauma–related behaviors.

EMDR: Eye Movement Desensitization and Reprocessing

EMDR is a modality that focuses upon helping the reprocessing of stored memories of traumatic events that infringe upon health and mental health. It involves a reformat of the brain's information-processing system of traumatic material regardless of the time period that may have elapsed since the event. Grounded in the Adaptive Information Processing (AIP) model (Shapiro and Laliotis, 2011), EMDR posits that traumatic memories are not fully possessed. New experiences are neurologically processed by one's memory processing system that has been negatively altered by unresolved traumatic memories. Thus one's informational processing system is impaired. As a result these unprocessed traumatic memories, and influencing thoughts and emotions, cause distress and impair one's strength and ability to move beyond the traumatizing event. Unsettling and traumatic memories are stored in the brain and easily triggered by a similar thought or experience repeatedly. This results in a response (behaviors) that dominates and overshadows any positive thoughts, behaviors, and emotions and impedes efforts of the individual to distance him- or herself and move forward.

EMDR practitioners utilizing the AIP model, assess the client's current symptoms and their perceptions, and inability to adapt and process current information. Shapiro and Laliotis (2011) state that the EMDR technique targets frozen memories allowing them to fully process. EMDR is a multiphase detailed treatment approach. The practitioner obtains a history from the client identifying positive and negative factors from their life. They move then to preparing and educating the client regarding the EMDR process, and reinforcing their strengths and control. When the practitioner has identified a specific target, a negatively held belief, and the desired positive belief, the reprocessing phase begins. This entails some sensory activity (eye movement following an object, tapping, or listening to a tone) while the client discusses their past distressing event. Upon completion of this process, the desensitization process is initiated, thus allowing positive experiences to also process and adapt. Beyond the desensitization intervention, the practitioner further emphasizes the client's positive cognitive thoughts and beliefs while further assessing for any unresolved residual symptoms. This may take upward of three sessions and once completed the process of termination and re-evaluation is conducted (Shapiro, 2007; Shapiro and Laliotis, 2011).

Since being introduced to the clinical profession, EMDR has established itself as efficacious for grief work. Following EMDR, clients were better able to access positive memories of their loved ones (Maxfield, 2009). Yet further research is needed to support the use of EMDR compared to other evidenced-based treatment approaches utilized for PTSD. Edmond, *et al.* (1999) conducted a randomized control study of female survivors of childhood trauma (sexually abused) who were assigned to three treatment groups (EMDR, routine, and delayed). The routine group participants were provided a variety of treatment modalities and techniques. The outcome of the EMDR treatment group showed clinical significance in reducing trauma symptoms among adult female survivors of childhood sexual abuse and a 50 percent decrease of negative beliefs of the sexual abuse post-treatment. The authors further support the use of this modality given the statistically significant decrease in targeted traumatic memories compared to the participants who received routine treatments. As encouraging as they were, the results did not definitively support EMDR as opposed to routine individual treatment based upon the outcomes of the standardized tests used in this study.

Inoue (2009) looked beyond just the resolution or reduction of symptoms of PTSD to a broader view of cognitions. This study examines whether EMDR benefitted improvement in cognitive functioning in addition to PTSD symptom reduction. Using a case–study approach, the author noted improvement in emotional tolerance, social relationships, coping, and cognitive abilities occurred with symptom reduction following EMDR. Yet this may not be solely attributable to EMDR as similar outcomes occur with other therapies as well. Yet through the years of its application for individuals who survived childhood trauma, Eye Movement Desensitization and Reprocessing modality continues to be utilized nationally and internationally. Trained EMDR practitioners were involved in the Humanitarian Assistance Program (HAP) along with International Relief Teams (IRT) and the Sri Lankan National Counselors Association (SRILNAC) to train counselors in EMDR in order to treat children and adult survivors of the tsunami of 2004. Outcome measures of these efforts were provided in qualitative terms given the restrictions of the contract with the Sri Lanka government. The pre-test and post-test measures reported an improvement of PTSD symptoms for survivors provided EMDR (Errebo, *et al.*, 2008).

In cases where symptoms beyond those noted for PTSD were present, EMDR also showed evidence in reducing those symptoms. Farrell, *et al.* (2010) measured the impact of EMDR in reducing trauma symptoms effects of sexual abuse by Roman Catholic priests. Research participants had previous psychotherapy, either psychodynamic or person-centered, prior to their inclusion in this study. In the initial Phase I (history taking), strengths as well as positive memories related to one's faith were important to obtain so as to avoid difficulty in successful completion of Phase IV (desensitization). It was further noted that themes such as theology and spirituality are used in the process of fully resolving blocked memories. The findings of this study were encouraging.

EMDR been reported to assist adults who survived childhood trauma and has enough efficacy research to be considered evidenced-based in reducing symptoms of PTSD. Yet research should, and is continuing to, further define long-term sustained relief from symptoms equal to other established evidence-based modalities such as Cognitive Behavioral Therapy.

Dialectical Behavior Therapy

There is extensive literature that associates childhood trauma with personality disorders, particularly Borderline Personality Disorder (BPD) (Haller and Miles, 2004; Allen and Lauterbach, 2007). Persons diagnosed with BPD exhibit patterns of impulsive behavior, mood instability, difficulty sustaining relationships, and a disorganized sense-of-self (American Psychiatric Association, 2000). Dialectical Behavior Therapy (DBT) was initially developed to assist individuals who met the criteria of Borderline Personality Disorder and were chronically suicidal (Linehan, *et al.*, 1991; Linehan, 1993; Dimeff and Linehan, 2001). DBT is a manualized treatment utilizing the basic concepts of Cognitive Behavioral Therapy but adding an emphasis on acceptance of the client's current abilities. Techniques focus on both acceptance and change and include skill training, contingency management, cognitive modification, and exposure to emotional cues.

DBT is a structured and intensive approach that involves individual and group (skills) therapy, as well as telephone contact, or coaching. Clients are seen for a minimum of one year in individual and group sessions. They are taught skills of mindfulness, interpersonal effectiveness, emotional regulation, and distress tolerance. The therapist is the lead in sessions, phone calls, or coaching if suicidal thoughts or plans become active for the client.

DBT has four targets, or stages, to assist clients in acquiring a better life and purpose (Swales, *et al.*, 2000; Dimeff and Linehan, 2001). The initial stage (I) focuses upon reducing and eliminating life-threatening behaviors such as suicide attempts. The second stage (II) focuses upon assisting clients from experiencing their feelings without avoiding life and isolating. The third stage (III) works toward building acceptance of the routine challenges of one's daily life such as employment and financial difficulties as well as relationship distress. The last stage (IV) assists clients with seeking completeness or a spiritual connection to fill any personal void.

While this modality had initially focused upon parasuicidal behaviors of persons diagnosed with Borderline Personality Disorder, it has found validity for adult survivors of childhood trauma who have an inability to regulate their emotions. Sweezy (2011) posits that people with emotional dysregulation may have experienced childhood trauma that was the result of a discrepancy between the temperaments of the caretaker and child. This, coupled with responding to challenged feelings with anxiety, fear, shame, and guilt can often lead not only to behaviors such as suicidal plans and gestures to avoid the feelings or emotionally deregulate but also difficulty in maintaining nurturing relationships. The author found that DBT group skills provided the client with the opportunity to counterbalance intense negative feelings.

Steil, *et al.* (2011) developed an approach to assist individuals who are survivors of childhood abuse that combines DBT and TF-CBT. The method includes individual and group sessions focused upon repairing self-esteem, mindfulness, and psychoeducation. In addition, the authors also introduced exposure techniques. Upon completion of this multimodal approach, the symptoms of PTSD were reduced.

Chapter 7

Military veterans and trauma

It is difficult to determine data on military veterans from a global perspective; there is not a standardized method of collecting and coding this information. Logic would dictate that the countries with the highest defense budgets would also have a proportional amount of war veterans. According to NATO (2011) reports, the United States spends more on defense than all of the European NATO countries combined. According to the US Census Bureau (2012), in 2011 there were 21.5 million living veterans, nationwide; of those, 9.2 million were over the age of 65 and 1.6 million were female. Sadly, the number of veterans with service-connected disabilities was 3.5 million with 810,245 have service-connected ratings of 70 percent or higher. In 2011, 476,515 veterans with PTSD received treatment through Veterans Affairs (VA) hospitals or clinics (US Department of Veterans Affairs, 2012). Though these reports are from the United States, there are likely proportionate findings across the globe.

These data demonstrate the urgency for a trauma-informed perspective when working with military veterans. A study of Australian Vietnam veterans revealed that 30 years after combat exposure, veterans had higher rates of long-term health problems when compared to the general population in Australia, and 50 percent took medication for at least one mental disorder (O'Toole, *et al.*, 2009).

As we have previously discussed, the research suggests the role of the hippocampus for encoding memories, and how that function may be inhibited and altered as a result of cumulative trauma exposure. This neural basis for understanding memory expands the cognitive model and helps us understand some of the confounding challenges combat veterans endure. Trauma memories may lack contextual detail and appear disjointed. Persons with PTSD appear to have neurological correlates that help us understand the symptoms they experience. The interplay between the amygdala, the hippocampus, and the prefrontal cortex is complex, and appears to adapt to stressors (Brown, et al., 1999; Sapolsky, et al., 2000; LeDoux, 2012). This adaptation, while essential for survival in the short-term, is detrimental when over-activated.

Utilizing fMRI technology, Hayes, et al. (2010) examined the neural basis of traumatic memory encoding in combat veterans with PTSD. Their findings revealed reduced hippocampal activity related to item-specific memories. They also noted that higher amygdala activity appeared to correlate with reduced hippocampal activity. These findings suggest that during times of extreme stress, humans create "gist" memories rather than specific detailed memories. Gist memories are memory snippets of an event; but the lack of detail, according to some researchers, can contribute to greater false-alarm triggers because threat becomes generalized rather than specific (Resick and Schnicke, 1992). Treatments that encourage more specific detail related to a trauma experience appear to help trauma survivors better contextualize (place in appropriate time and place) trauma memory which results in reduction in anxiety symptoms (Resick and Schnicke, 1992; Foa, et al., 2009; McLean and Foa, 2011).

In a longitudinal neuroimaging study of changes in brain anatomy related to PTSD (Cardenas, et al., 2011), the brain volume of 25 military veterans who had been diagnosed with PTSD, and 22 veterans who did not have PTSD were recorded. Using MRI scans, both groups were examined at baseline, then again 24 months later. Over time, 11 of the subjects with PTSD improved and their trauma symptoms had reduced. Their scans did not show any significant brain atrophy when compare to those without PTSD. However, the subgroup of veterans whose PTSD symptoms continued over time showed accelerated atrophy in the brainstem, frontal and temporal regions of the brain. Bremner, et al. (1999) utilized a PET scan to examine the neural correlates of distress in a study with combat veterans with PTSD. Their findings revealed that after exposure to traumatic pictures, there was decreased blood flow to the medial prefrontal cortex; the area understood to be instrumental in cognitive behavior, decision making, and moderating behavior.

Within the neuroscience community, there have been some interesting findings that will generate further research. For instance, not all neuroscience research supports that trauma is causal in hippocampal atrophy. In a study by Gilbertson, et al. (2002), combat veterans with severe PTSD showed smaller hippocampal volumes than their non-combat exposed peers. What is interesting about this study, it that the subjects were all monozygotic twins. When the hippocampal volumes of the non-combat twins were measured, they too revealed decreased volume, comparable to their trauma-exposed twins. These data may indicate that hippocampal volume may be pre-existing, familial, and vulnerable for sensitivity to stress-related disorders.

Data on treatment outcomes for veterans with PTSD come from a large body of research focused on cognitive behavioral treatments. In a report to the Veterans Administration in the US, CBT was cited to be the most efficacious in treating PTSD (Institute of Medicine, 2007). EMDR, Prolonged Exposure therapy (PE), and Cognitive Processing Therapy, draw from the theoretical context of CBT (Schnurr and Friedman, 2008). Although there is little data that supports the efficacy of group treatment in treating PTSD, it is widely utilized, and when combined with Cognitive Processing Therapy, there appears to be some validity for its use (Chard, *et al.*, 2010). While there are numerous other treatment methods being used to treat trauma survivors, the modalities included in this chapter have the support of a growing body of literature that is congruent with a trauma-informed approach to care and findings from neuroscience.

Treatment for military veterans

Posttraumatic stress disorder and comorbid mental health disorders, resulting from exposure to trauma, occurs in less than 8 percent of the general population of the United States. However, nearly 31 percent of US veterans who served in the Vietnam War reported a lifetime prevalence of combat-related PTSD. To date 17 percent of Iraq and Afghanistan combat veterans have been diagnosed with a trauma-related disorder (Marmar, 2009). An improved approach by the US Department of Defense (DOD) and Department of Veterans Affairs (VA) to provide mental health treatment is occurring for veterans of Iraq and Afghanistan, an effort that did not occur for those returning from the Vietnam War. Part of the improved effort is to screen veterans for PTSD criteria after they exit the war zone, and then again several months later. If treatment is indicated, evidence-based treatment modalities are provided by trained practitioners. Treatment methods primarily utilized by the VA are Cognitive Behavioral Therapy (CBT) with the incorporation of imaginal and in vivo exposure, and Cognitive Processing Therapy, which addresses irrational beliefs, related to traumatic exposure (Marmar, 2009). While the screening for PTSD is not perfected, given the variables involved, improved access to mental health services for the veteran population because of research is a movement in the right direction. The following section outlines specifics for evidence-based treatment methods that have demonstrated efficacy in working with military veterans with trauma-related symptoms. Table 7.1 provides an overview of several treatment methods that appear to demonstrate efficacy in sustained symptom reduction for treating military veterans suffering from PTSD.

Psychopharmacology

Symptoms of PTSD are invasive and cause distress in social and occupational function. Nightmares about the traumatic event, panic, isolation, disruptive thoughts, avoidance of trauma reminders, and impulsive reactions to others often interfere with a veteran's transitioning post-combat. Interruption in quality of life from these symptoms can often lead to increased difficulties in lifestyle, such as substance abuse and complex mental health problems. The use of psychopharmacology is one method used for treating PTSD (National Center for PTSD, 2007). While the utilization of medications is not considered to be the sole treatment for PTSD, many of the recommended agents provide relief from symptom interference and, therefore, using medication is often an initial approach to treatment. Medications such as Fluoxetine, Paroxetin and Sertraline are SSRIs, and have demonstrated to be the most effective, are fast-acting, and responsive within two to four weeks of treatment. Serotonin and norepinephrine reuptake inhibitors (SNRIs) such as Venlafaxine have also been useful in symptom reduction (Ipser and Stein, 2012). The efficacy of SSRI and SNRI medication has been demonstrated in treating combat veterans with symptoms of avoidance, depression, and anxiety related to PTSD (Foa, et al., 2009; Avedisova, 2011).

Recent focus upon the neurobiological process of disrupted sleep associated with PTSD has shown some promise. While researching the psychopharmacological influence upon the symptoms of PTSD, Lydiard and Hamner (2009) identified the interruption of REM sleep as having clinical importance in understanding symptoms alterations in arousal and reactivity found in the diagnostic criterion (Criterion E) for PTSD (American Psychiatric Association, 2000). These symptoms, included in this study, were: hyperarousal, difficulty falling and staying asleep, and hypervigilance. Difficulty falling and staying asleep, in particular, is thought to be a result of changes in the amygdala and other mid-brain activity as a result trauma. Persons with PTSD tend to sleep lightly and have difficulty reaching the REM sleep state (Caldwell and Redeker, 2005). According to research, disruption in the noradrenergic system will likely interrupt the REM sleep process. This in turn leads to frequent wakening and sleep disturbances (Lydiard and Hamner, 2009). Prazosin, a long-standing antihypertensive agent, has shown promise in addressing intrusive symptoms,

Table 7.1 Examples of trauma-informed treatment for military veterans

	Treatment focus			
	Fear extinction	Emotion regulation	Attentional/cognitive restructuring	Relational
Cognitive Behavioral Therapy	Techniques that facilitate fear extinction.	Cognitive restructuring to regulate emotionality.	Techniques that identify trauma cues and assist in restructuring maladaptive cognitive distortions.	Allows for symptom reduction which provides, in part, ability for social engagement.
Prolonged Exposure therapy	Reduces fear of the traumatic event by redefining the event as it occurred but within the context of current time.	Use of in vivo (direct) and imagery (indirect) exposure.	Assists in identifying negative cognitions and use of reprocessing of that event with imagery.	Symptom reduction improves social relationships. Group process promotes social skill building.
Cognitive Processing Therapy	Techniques that facilitate fear extinction.	Detailing the experience, diminishing the impact of related emotions.	Uses exposure therapy with an emphasis to disprove maladaptive beliefs, reduces self-blame.	Symptom reduction can improve social engagement with others.
Virtual Reality Exposure	Controlled, computerized technology to generate a simulated experience in a safe setting.	Clinician-controlled simulated exposure to trauma situations reduced symptoms of depression and anxiety.	Controlled exposure to simulated trauma toward reduction of maladaptive thoughts and behaviors.	Symptom reduction can improve social engagement with others.
Seeking Safety	Main focus is upon feeling of safety in relationships, thinking, behavior, and emotions.	Emphasis on safety in all areas of life.	Main content areas of treatment include cognitive, behavioral, interpersonal, and case management.	Occurs in groups which allows for social support and engagement.
Eye Movement Desensitization and Reprocessing (EMDR)	Conducted in a safe and therapeutic environment by trained clinician.	Techniques that move unprocessed negative emotionally charged memory into long-term memory.	Integrated techniques for cognitive and behavioral restructuring related to trauma.	Symptom reduction can improve social engagement with others.

such as nightmares, during sleep. In military personnel, and others with insomnia and/or disrupted sleep, Prazosin administered at bedtime in graduated and monitored dosing, has shown to reduce nightmares (Germain, et al., 2012; Lydiard and Hamner, 2009). While symptom reduction achieved by medication offers symptom relief in PTSD, it does little to alter any structural changes that may have occurred because of trauma. As we know, the brain is a patterning organ and use-dependent (Perry, 2006); therefore, medication alone addresses only part of the complex cluster of symptom evidenced in persons with PTSD.

Cognitive Behavior Therapy

The US Department of Veterans Affairs (VA) has made public their initiatives to address the high incidence of PTSD in returning combat veterans. The National Center for PTSD, created by the VA, provides comprehensive information on PTSD targeting the public, veterans, and professionals. For treatment, the VA provides two CBT approaches to treating veterans with PTSD, Cognitive Processing Therapy (CPT) and Prolonged Exposure (PE) therapy (National Center for PTSD, 2007).

CBT is the treatment of choice in most published guidelines for treating PTSD and is recommended for use to resolve fear based memories, avoidant behaviors and problematic beliefs. Techniques utilized in CBT are demonstrated to facilitate fear extinction and assist in restructuring maladaptive cognitive distortions related to trauma. Cognitive distortions refer to erroneous views, perceptions, and memories of traumatic events that continue to occur long past the event has ended. The core emphasis of this method is to challenge, or dispute, the client's negative thinking, and then provide strategies to restructure the thought process. In a comprehensive review of efficacy outcomes using CBT, Mendes, et al. (2008) examined findings from 23 clinical trials that used CBT to treat persons with PTSD. Collectively, the study subjects were comprised of 898 patients in treatment groups and 1,025 in control groups. The structures used in the 23 studies were:

- four utilized brief individual sessions (four or fewer sessions)
- 17 utilized prolonged individual sessions (more than four)
- one utilized group CBT alone
- one utilized group CBT combined with two individual sessions.

The findings from this comparative meta-analysis revealed that CBT was more effective than EMDR in remission of PTSD symptoms. The analysis of CBT and exposure therapy outcomes revealed that both methods were equally effective in diagnostic remission. The examination of outcomes between CBT and supportive therapies reveal that CBT is more effective in remission of PTSD symptoms.

The CBT approach has expanded since its inception (Beck, 1991) and can be subdivided into by various techniques utilized. *Cognitive* uses cognitive restructuring; *behavioral* adds behavioral components, such as in vivo exposure in Prolonged Exposure therapy. EMDR, group CBT, mindfulness, and Cognitive Processing Therapy are all subsets of CBT (Mendes, *et al.*, 2008).

Prolonged Exposure Therapy

Prolonged Exposure therapy (PE) was developed by Edna Foa and is highly effective in reducing clinical symptoms of PTSD. PE was one of only two therapies selected by the VA to be expanded across their system (Sharpless and Barber, 2011). McLean and Foa (2011) posit that recovery from traumatic events includes repetitive exposure to the trauma-based stimuli so as to activate fear. The difference between this approach and traditional supportive therapy (where clients continue to relive their trauma experience and emotions) is the cognitive component. Additional retelling the story of the traumatic event assists with defining the event as it occurred but within the context of current time. This assists in identifying negative cognitions that support the fearful memory of the event. Prolonged Exposure, a form of CBT, is conducted in a series of 9–15 sessions, encompassing three main elements. The first element is *in vivo exposure*, which is direct confrontation of reminders of the trauma experience, such as activities or objects. The second element is *imaginal* exposure to the memory of that event. This is accomplished repeatedly recounting the traumatic event. The final element is the *cognitive processing* of the imagined event (Foa and Kozak, 1986; McLean and Foa, 2011).

In vivo exposure is the technique used for real-time confrontation with the feared stimuli. Together with the client, the practitioner establishes a hierarchy of fear and avoidance situations and then the client is given exposure to these triggers as "homework." Imaginal exposure occurs when the client imagines him or herself experiencing the feared stimuli and verbally describes the imagination during a session. As the client envisions what is feared, they describe what they are imagining in detail and in a present tense form. For example, they might say "I am walking toward the area where I pitched the grenade." etc. It is believed that continued detailed revelation of the imagined feared stimuli reduces the impact of that fear and the emotions associated with it. Insight is gained as the client comes to know that they are not in the *event*, nor is the event occurring in the present. As awareness solidifies for the client, other symptoms, such as, isolation, guilt feelings, and survivor's guilt associated with PTSD also diminish. Positive reinforcement from the practitioner, incorporation of new information obtained from the session, and use of rating scales all assist in determining the change in the client level of disturbance.

One significant symptom that distinguishes PTSD of combat veterans from others is that of compulsive checking. Clients have reported checking under cars or in their yards for explosive devices, in multiple and repetitive manners. This behavior often interferes with their routines, sleep patterns, and relationships with other. Tuerk, *et al.* (2009) report cases findings where PE treatment successfully reduced this compulsive behavior.

The US Department of Defense and the Department of Veteran Affairs have supported the use of PE. Many mental health practitioners in the VA have been, and are being, trained in this modality and more are needed. In support of continued training of practitioners in this modality, a recent study of active military service women meeting the criteria of PTSD and seeking treatment was conducted. A randomized clinical study of PTSD treatment for women who are in active-duty military utilizing PE and Present Centered Therapy was conducted (Schnurr, *et al.*, 2007). Within the sample, 70 percent of the service women reported sexual trauma. The presenting symptomology was similar in both treatment groups. The findings of the study indicated improvement of symptom reduction in both groups; however, the outcomes were more favorable for those who received PE treatment.

The VA continues to research the benefit of this modality to the veteran client. A recent study found that a significant portion of clients completed at least seven sessions, or terminated treatment prior to the seventh session due to clinical improvement. Those who received PE utilized less mental health services with a reduced per person cost of services, than those who did not. However, those who did not complete the treatment protocol used more mental health services, thus increasing the cost of those services by 17 percent (Tuerk, *et al.*, 2012).

Cognitive Processing Therapy

Initially developed by Resick and Schnicke (1992) to treat symptoms of PTSD in rape victims, Cognitive Processing Therapy (CPT) makes use of exposure therapy with the additional focus of providing factual information to disprove distorted and maladaptive beliefs associated with the traumatic event(s). According to Resick and Schnicke, recovery by exposure to traumatic memories alone was insufficient, and did not provide for cognitive restructuring. CPT makes use of exposure therapy with the additional focus of providing factual information to disprove distorted and maladaptive beliefs associated with the traumatic event(s).

This modality has been utilized in residential programs for veterans diagnosed with PTSD (Alvarez, *et al.*, 2011; Zappert and Westrup, 2008). Research findings indicate a clinically significant decrease in presenting symptoms of PTSD after receiving CPT. Despite the complexity of veterans needing residential care, CPT treatment appears to be well tolerated (Alvarez, *et al.*, 2011) and effective in countering not only symptoms of PTSD, but distorted, self-blaming thoughts as well (Zappert and Westrup, 2008).

Studies, mostly conducted in collaboration with the VA report similar positive findings (Monson, *et al.*, 2006; Chard, *et al.*, 2010; Cigrang, *et al.*, 2011). According to Sharpless and Barber (2011), CPT, along with PE, is being expanded by the VA as a treatment choice for PTSD.

Virtual Reality Exposure

Capitalizing on new technologies, Virtual Reality Exposure Therapy (VRET) uses computer-generated simulation of their trauma experience during exposure therapy and may be useful for clients who have difficulty visualizing the trauma memory that is predominant in their symptomatology. The session is conducted in a therapist's office in a controlled multidimensional simulation of that event. In this modality, the client is exposed to the situation as if he/she was present. Using a computerized virtual environment, the client wears a head-mounted display with position tracker and headphones. Simulated images and audio are presented to the client providing the client with a real time experience (Rothbaum, *et al.*, 1999; Opris, *et al.*, 2012).

Opris, *et al.* (2012) provided a meta-analysis of published research comparing the use of VRET to reduce anxiety in the general population. The authors analyzed 23 research articles comparing this modality to that of other evidence-based treatments such as CBT, CPT and exposure therapy. The results showed comparable significant reduction in anxiety for participants in all treatment groups, with one exception; those with a fear of flying responded much more favorably to VRET.

Technology utilized in VRET has advanced since its inception (Rizzo, *et al.*, 2011). The computer-simulated virtual experience can be displayed for a client by way of various technologies that present real-time simulation of the remembered event including 3D, audio, and olfactory simulation.

The Institute for Creative Technologies at the University of Southern California has spearheaded virtual platforms such as Virtual Iraq and Virtual Afghanistan scenarios, and the Stress Resilience in Virtual Environments (STRIVE) project. The latter is designed to promote resiliency and coping strategies for service members prior to their deployment to combat fronts. The Department of Defense has promoted the use of this program throughout the military (Rizzo et al., 2011).

The use of VRET with veteran combat service members has been conducted in the United States and Europe. These studies have involved former combat veterans who are diagnosed with PTSD from the Vietnam War, Iraq, Afghanistan, and Portugal's war in Africa over 30 years ago. In a pilot project, veteran service members of the Portugal military were treated with VRET to decrease symptoms of PTSD that had sustained 30 years post-combat (Gamito, *et al.*, 2010). Three groups of veteran Portuguese service members were randomly assigned to three subject groups, VRET, Exposure Imagination (EI) therapy, or wait-listed (WL). Those in the VRET and EI groups received 12 sessions. The findings indicated a lessening of symptoms of depression and anxiety for those who received VRET and EI with the VRET group responding slightly better than the EI group. The WL group had some reduction in symptoms but note they were not statistically significant.

Use of this method for treating members of active service post-combat is beginning to emerge in the literature. Tworus, *et al.* (2010) present a case study of a soldier who escaped death three times while on tour in Iraqi. Upon his second hospitalization for severe PTSD symptoms, he engaged in a treatment of VRET. His symptoms improved to such an extent, he was able to return to military service. There is additional evidence of the effectiveness of VRET for active service members in combat settings demonstrated in a study of veterans who had served at least one tour of combat duty in Operation Iraqi Freedom (OIF) or Operation Enduring Freedom (OEF) (Reger, *et al.*, 2011). The subjects in the study had a current diagnosis of PTSD and experienced limited improvement in their condition from traditional psychotherapy. The Virtual Iraqi environment was utilized using head-mounted visual display equipment with audio speakers and olfactory stimulation. The participants were presented with 12 sessions; the average completion was seven sessions. Those receiving at least seven sessions of VRET experienced clinically significant reductions of their symptoms of PTSD (Reger, *et al.*, 2011).

In a similar research study of active service members diagnosed with PTSD (McLay, *et al.*, 2012), participants received VRET utilizing a head set with audio. The therapist was able to control stimuli in each of the 12–15 sessions. Of the initial 42 participants, 20 participants completed the course of treatment. Of those 20 completers, 75 percent no longer met the clinical criteria for PTSD with at least a 50 percent improvement noted. There was also reduction in symptoms of depression and anxiety, which was sustained at the three-month post-treatment assessment. These initial research findings are promising for the technologically supported method of using VRET for active service members diagnosed with PTSD.

Group Treatment

While CBT is commonly used in individual treatment, it is also effective in a group session program as well. Sharpless and Barber (2011) found that CBT Group Treatment provided to over 600 military service personnel resulted in significant reduction of PTSD symptoms. Variations of CBT have developed, with some success, for use in group setting.

Seeking Safety is a treatment group developed by Lisa Najavits for treating PTSD and substance abuse disorders under a grant from the National Institute of Drug Abuse grant. Over time, it has been applied to treatment with other populations as well (Najavits, 2009). Seeking Safety is a 25-session manual-guided CBT approach with feelings of safety as its primary goal. The format can be used for individuals or groups. Each of the 25 topics have related *safe coping skills* and address cognitive, behavioral, interpersonal, or case management domains. The model has five key principles:

1   Safety from substance abuse, dangerous relationships, and self-harming behavior.
2   Utilization of an integrated treatment approach to PTSD and substance abuse.
3   Focus on returning the client to a state of a hopeful view of their future.
4   Attention to cognition, behaviors, and interpersonal abilities (general case management needs).
5   Self-care for the practitioner.

Co-occurring disorders are not uncommon with military veterans, especially combat veterans, and often present barriers to recovery. Seeking Safety has shown to be effective for veterans with comorbid diagnoses. Several studies report decreased PTSD and Substance Use Disorder symptoms for veteran participants in the Seeking Safety group program (Desai, et al., 2008; Norman, et al., 2010). The structure of Seeking Safety provides a clearly articulated treatment approach that has gained popularity in a variety of settings and certainly holds promise for expansion for working with veterans.

Trauma Focus Group Therapy (TFGT) includes the basic constructs of individual exposure therapy but expands it to group treatment settings. The group model focuses upon improving one's self-control and quality of life with symptom reduction (Foy, et al., 2002). TFGT emphasizes prolonged exposure, cognitive restructuring, and relapse prevention, with a greater emphasis on exposure to war-related trauma experiences.

TFGT is delivered in 30 weekly sessions. The sessions are divided into three categories of focus: introductory or educational work, war-zone related, and relapse prevention. Each group session includes check in, homework, and checkout, then specific topics for group discussion. Homework is a key element to this model and designed to close any gap between the group sessions and the day-to-day lives of the group members. Homework extends the benefit of the group session beyond the doors of the group room (Foy, et al., 2002).

The sessions referred to as "introductory" primarily focus on educating the group members on the treatment process, the signs and symptoms of PTSD disorder, coping strategies, and an awareness of how they may respond during the group treatment process. The war-zone sessions are typically two hours in length, audiotaped. and begin with the description of a trauma scene and proceeds onto systematic exposure. As the group members experience the memory of this trauma, the systemic exposure is designed to reduce the fears and memory, while strengthening coping ability. With the description of the trauma, cognitive distortions are identified and challenged by the members. Homework − listening to the audiotaped session − in this phase is to improve the members' ability to re-experience the trauma while reducing the fears associated with the event. The third phase of this model is relapse prevention which also includes termination from treatment. This phase focuses upon empowering one's ability to anticipate future challenges in daily life by identifying potential risks in situations, enforcing and using coping strategies, and their overall treatment experience.

EMDR

As discussed in an earlier chapter, Eye Movement Desensitization and Reprocessing (EMDR) is based upon the concept that some stored memories, especially traumatic ones, are not fully processed by the brain. The unprocessed material interferes with future experiences as a result of the faulty memory processing system (Russell, *et al.*, 2007). By adapting information-processing techniques, EMDR integrates the negative behavioral memory, that is still in a "raw state" and moves it into long-term memory that can consider context, such as the past (Silver, *et al.*, 2008).

Combat veterans can suffer from complex PTSD as a result of experiencing multiple traumas. Members of the military are trained to respond to threat and see, hear, and smell the elements of combat daily. This sensory assault sets the tone for complex PTSD. Because EMDR focuses on sensory integration it has potential to be used immediately, in the field (Silver, *et al.*, 2008). During the treatment session(s) should a painful experience become known, rather than discuss or reveal it the client will state a reference to that experience. The practitioner will direct the client's attention to that area and continue the stimulation technique allowing for resolution beyond these barriers (Salvatore, 2009; Silver, *et al.*, 2008).

It was only after the Vietnam War that the cluster of symptoms we now call PTSD was studied in any great depth. According to Ruzek, *et al.* (2007), treatment goals for returning veterans are specific:

- prevent family breakdown
- prevent social withdrawal and isolation
- prevent employment problems
- prevent alcohol and substance abuse.

This chapter has provided some strategies toward these goals that have demonstrated encouraging efficacy data. It appears that, as a species, humans are destined to make war against each other. However, it is not the members of the military who make these decisions. They obey when they are called. Therefore assisting the men and women of the military as they return home should be a principal focus within any government who called them to serve in the first place.

Chapter 8

Trauma experienced in adulthood

Traumatic events can occur at any time during one's life cycle. In earlier chapters, we discussed the impact of trauma on children, adult survivors of childhood trauma, and military veterans. The focus of this chapter is on the impact of trauma on adults. Because it has already been addressed, the literature included in this chapter excludes data on studies related to the cumulative effect of trauma from childhood. It is important to understand the neuroscience implications of trauma on a fully developed brain both conceptually and prognostically.

The types of trauma experienced in adulthood cover a broad range of tragedies. While there may be some differences in posttrauma recovery based upon the type of trauma experienced, the literature suggests that the nature – episodic versus chronic – of the trauma may better inform decisions in practice intervention. Included in this chapter is literature related to rape and sexual violence, interpersonal violence, violent crimes, and survivors of extreme natural disasters. In each subsection, treatment methods that demonstrate a trauma-informed focus are presented. By our definition, a trauma-informed focus includes strategies related to fear extinction, emotion regulation, attention and cognitive restructuring, and relationship strengthening.

Adult survivors of rape and sexual violence

Rape is a crime of rage and dominance, not a sex act. A study that collected crime statistics from 60 participating countries, conducted by the United Nations, revealed that rape was reported more than any other crime (Lewis, 1999). In the United States, females accounted for 94 percent of all rapes; 59 percent of those rapes reported to the police were also treated for injuries (Rennison, 2002). This is a crime that may disrupt a survivor's sense of safety and their sense of self-worth. In this subsection, we provide several comparative studies that measure treatment outcomes for adult survivors of rape and sexual violence.

As we have discussed in earlier chapters, trauma can disrupt fear-extinction systems that enable a person to return to non-threat state once the threat is no longer present. This dysfunction results in over-activity in the hypothalamic-pituitary-adrenal (HPA) axis (Yehuda, 2002). In this state, the brain continues to sense threat and triggers corticotrophin releasing hormones (CRH) and adrenocorticotropic hormones (ACTH) to respond, which then releases cortisol into the bloodstream. In persons with PTSD, cortisol reactivity appears to be different from persons with anxiety (Yehuda, 2006). Gerardi, *et al.* (2010) conducted a study of salivary cortisol levels in female rape victims following two methods of treatment. The participants had all experienced rape three months or longer prior to the study. Seventy-four participants were randomly assigned to either PE or EMDR treatment groups or wait-listed (WL) as the control group. Both treatment groups received nine 90-minute sessions twice a week. Upon completion, the findings revealed that participants in both treatment groups demonstrated decreased PTSD symptoms that were significantly higher than those in WL. Between the PE and EMDR groups, there was not a significant comparative difference in outcomes; both were effective. In those participants who experienced a 50 percent or larger reduction in PTSD symptoms, cortisol values were significantly lower following treatment. The researchers hypothesize that the avoidance behaviors noted in posttrauma survivors appear to aggravate the stress response in the brain. Both PE and EMDR target avoidances as a treatment goal.

In addition to dysregulation in the fear circuitry following rape trauma, cognitive distortions related to the rape are not uncommon. Shame and self-blame are frequently reported residual symptoms of rape and sexual assault. Feelings of shame may serve as a significant barrier to trauma recovery in adult survivors. These feelings represent cognitive distortions that keep a person tied to the event (Van Vliet, 2008). In a study to assess self-blame, counterfactual thinking, and well-being in rape survivors, Branscombe, *et al.* (2003) determined that self-blame has a negative impact on well-being. They recommend that treatment that focuses on the specific behaviors that occurred during the assault be viewed as contributing to survival rather than what the survivor could have done to avoid the attack. The relationship to the rape perpetrator may also impede treatment efforts in adult survivors of rape and sexual assault. Assault by a stranger appears to have a greater negative impact over the long term on the well-being of a rape survivor than attack by a known perpetrator (Gutner, et al., 2006).

Cognitive Processing Therapy (CPT) was developed for treating survivors of rape who suffer from PTSD. CPT is based upon cognitive behavioral perspectives and introduces exposure therapy techniques. The intent of CPT is to integrate the memory of the traumatic event into long-term memory, to confront negative cognitive distortions and beliefs, and to regulate emotions (Green and Roberts, 2008). CPT is a manual-guided approach, generally consisting of 12 sessions. CPT uses narrative and cognitive interventions, and the exposure component is less rigorous than imaginal exposure therapy and may be more acceptable to clients who want an alternative to exposure therapy (ISTSS, 2013). Session topics include education on PTSD, a written narration of one's personal trauma, understanding the cognitive triad, Socratic questioning in effort to challenge negative thoughts and feelings, rewriting the trauma event, and retelling the event to the therapist with a focus on challenging and changing beliefs. Themes of trust, power, safety, self-esteem, and intimacy are a focal point at each session (Resick, et al., 2002).

A study involving women who had experienced recent sexual assault (Resick and Schnicke, 1992) examined the efficacy of CPT in reducing posttrauma symptoms in a group setting. The control group for the study was those on a wait-list for treatment. The 12-session process included information on PTSD at the initial session. In the second session, clients were to identify and distinguish feelings from thoughts involved in their traumatic event. Sessions three and four involved writing about their emotions and the event. The fifth session focused upon challenging negative beliefs. Session six involved understanding faulty thinking patterns. Sessions 7–11 continued challenging negative beliefs and began incorporating safety, trust, power, esteem, and intimacy. The final session was an overview of progress and future goals. After 12 group sessions, PTSD rating scales demonstrated reduction of symptoms in group participants.

Resick, et al. (2002) conducted a comparative study of PE and CPT to measure their impact on PTSD symptoms in female rape survivors. The control group for the study was those placed on a wait-list. At the end of the treatment course, findings revealed a significant reduction in PTSD symptoms in both treatment groups. Those on the wait-list for treatment did not experience any reduction in symptoms of PTSD. Longitudinal measures for each group were as follows:

- At the end of treatment: PTSD symptoms were evident in only 19.5 percent of the CPT treatment group and 17.5 percent of the PE treatment group.
- At the three-month follow-up, PTSD symptoms were evident in 16.2 percent of CPT and 29.7 percent of PE participants.
- At nine-month follow-up, PTSD symptoms were evident in 19.2 percent of the CPT treatment group and 15.4 percent of PE treatment group (Resick, *et al.*, 2012).

In a follow-up to the study cited above, 87.5 percent (n = 26) of the original study subjects were able to be contacted and reassessed an average of six years after the initial study (Resick, *et al.*, 2012). Findings from the six-year follow-up study revealed that within the CPT treatment group, PTSD symptoms were evident in 22.2 percent and in 17.5 percent of the PE treatment group. The sustained PTSD symptom remission six years after treatment is encouraging. At the time of the initial study, the women were in their thirties. Data collected in the final study revealed that in addition to diagnostic remission of PTSD, the subjects reported improved stability in their relationships and increased attainment in education goals (Resick, *et al.*, 2012).

Stress Inoculation Training (SIT) also draws from CBT concepts and has been used in treating adult survivors of rape and sexual assault (Foa, *et al.*, 1991). The focus of SIT is to gain greater understanding of how narratives, self-talk, and behaviors are associated with traumatic memories and may promote stress-related symptoms. Stress from traumatic events can disable and distance a trauma survivor from adaptive behaviors when faced with future stressful events (Meichenbaum, 2007). SIT is typically conducted in hour-long sessions over 8–15 weeks and by a follow-up session one year post-treatment.

The initial phase of SIT is focused upon engagement between the client and the therapist, establishing a relationship that, supported by trust, provides the platform for the client to conceptualize and confront their stressor. The focus then shifts to understanding stress, stress cues, and the removal of personal barriers to wellness, and the presentation of new coping skills. The final phase involves in vivo practice of newly acquired coping skills. SIT techniques include role playing, imagery, and practicing behaviors such as relaxation techniques.

Foa, *et al.* (1991) conducted a randomized controlled study of victims of rape. The participants were randomly assigned one of four groups:

- Prolonged Exposure (PE)
- Stress Inoculation Training (SIT)
- Supportive Counseling (SC)
- Wait-List (WL).

Each treatment group received nine sessions, twice weekly, for 4.5 weeks. Those on the WL received no treatment. The findings revealed that all participants experienced a reduction in PTSD symptoms at end of 4.5 weeks. Clinical significance occurred for those receiving PE (40 percent) and SIT (71 percent). Statistical significance was not obtained in SC (20 percent) or WL (18 percent).

PE therapy has been found to be an asset to assisting veterans in recovering from combat trauma as well as victims who have PTSD related to non-combat traumatic events (Miller,1998; Abou and Goldwaser, 2009; Resick, et al., 2012). Although PE is manualized, it is a flexible treatment approach for those who have been affected by trauma resulting in PTSD. It involves in vivo, direct, and monitored exposure to the real-life object of avoidance, and *imaginal* exposure where the person recalls, visualizes, and experiences the object of avoidance in thought only. The treatment includes several components of focus including education, trained breathing, actual, and imaginal exposure, and occurs across nine sessions (Resick, et al., 2002).

Positive outcomes when treating adult survivors of sexual assault have been noted in PE, CPT, EMDR, and SIT methods. Each of these methods addresses, at minimum, strategies related to feelings of safety, emotion regulation, and cognitive distortions related to the event.

Interpersonal violence

Interpersonal partner violence (IPV), also known as domestic violence, can have far-reaching and devastating effects on individuals and families. Studies on IPV both reveal health and mental health long-term and often intergenerational effects. In recent years, there has been an increase in research on IPV globally which gives insight into some cultural confounding issues. Worldwide, women are more at risk of being the recipient of violence when pregnant (Iliyasu, et al., 2013). Cultural norms that justify IPV have long been a contributor to IPV and were reinforced in two recent studies on domestic violence in India (Kimuna, et al., 2013; Stephenson, et al., 2013).

As we have noted in previous discussion, emotion regulation is a common residual effect of chronic exposure to fear and threat. The familial impact of domestic violence appears to affect mothers with interpersonal violence histories. A recent study (Schechter, *et al.*, 2013) revealed that mothers with interpersonal violence-related PTSD have increased activity within fear-circuitry systems compared to healthy controls. Utilizing fMRI technology, the study participants had higher activation in the fear-response circuitry and decreased activation in the higher cortical areas when observing videos of their children and other children in free play. The fMRI scans also revealed that the subjects had continued activity in the fear-response system once the stressor was removed. This information regarding dysfunction in fear extinction, emotion regulation, and decreased cortical activity is relevant for treatment selection when working with interpersonal trauma survivors.

In is not uncommon for women with a history of physical or sexual abuse to also have co-occurring mental and substance abuse disorders. The Women, Co-occurring Disorders, and Violence Study (WCDVS) sponsored by the Substance Abuse and Mental Health Services Agency, examined the effectiveness of treatment for women with co-occurring disorders and a history of interpersonal violence utilizing gender-specific, trauma-informed, and integrated approaches (McHugo, *et al.*, 2005). The WCDVS was a quasi-experimental longitudinal study. Prior to this study, there was little known data on the outcomes of utilizing integrated treatment models for treating women with co-occurring disorders and a history of physical or sexual violence. The women in the experimental group received integrated, trauma-informed, and CSR-involved services. For the purposes of this study, CSR is defined as consumers of mental health services (C), survivors of trauma (S), and women in recovery (R). The comparison group had access to services as usual. The women in the integrated experimental group demonstrated higher rates of symptom reduction than those who received general services.

EMDR has been utilized with some success in treating adult survivors of interpersonal violence. As described in Chapter 6, Eye Movement Desensitization and Reprocessing is grounded in the Adaptive Information Processing model (Shapiro and Laliotis, 2011). EMDR is a multiphased treatment approach where the practitioner identifies factors of the client's history, and targets a negatively held belief. The process of AIP is to allow for positive experiences to be fully processed and adapted. This process is augmented with cognitive interventions to sustain the positive thinking and clear any unresolved residual symptoms.

While there is not a large body of literature on EMDR, findings to date have been encouraging. In a study with a small sample of participants who survived an intimate partner rape, Tarquinio, *et al.* (2012) participants were assessed using quantitative and qualitative instruments during pre-treatment and post-treatment sessions. Participants were assessed for PTSD symptom presentation. Outcomes revealed clinically significant outcomes by self-report in symptom reduction for all participants. Symptoms related to depression anxiety, and PTSD no longer met the APA diagnostic rigor for PTSD.

Trauma and violent crime

Exposure to violence crimes impacts an essential component of well-being, safety. Whether a person lives in high-crime areas related to poverty, territorial strife, or drugs, or is the victim of a random violent act, safety is disrupted. Depending on the chronicity of the exposure, the meaning of the event, and related losses, recovery can be a challenge. One method for treating victims of crime is Narrative Therapy. Narrative Therapy helps solidify fragmented components of a trauma experience so that it is better understood (White and Epston, 1990; White, 2003), and introduce and solidify the components of one's experience so that they are better understood when organized with meaning. To tell one's story in a manner that is separate from the person best allows an objective view of the experience and helps clients learn to distance and differentiate themselves from the experience.

Mashiach, *et al.* (2004) compared various styles of coping by way of narratives of five men who experienced the same traumatic event. Use of the narrative modality providing insight to the person's perception of what occurred (ambush with shootings and injuries) differed among the survivors. These differences were attributed to personality, situational factors, physical injury, and/or past traumas. Over a four-month period, the narratives of these individuals were compared for benevolence, meaningfulness, and self-worth. The results showed that with an organized narrative reflecting one's coherent story and a positive self-image, the symptoms of PTSD lessened (Mashiach, *et al.*, 2004).

Seeking Safety, described in detail in Chapter 7, is a cognitive restructuring treatment model with a goal of resolving the effects of trauma exposure coupled with co-occurring substance abuse by the victim. Seeking Safety has four concentration areas of treatment focus, cognitive, behavioral, interpersonal, and case management (Najavits, 2009). Twenty-five themes pertaining to coping strategies and restructuring cognition are utilized across the length of the program. Seeking Safety appears to be effective with several types of trauma and co-occurring substance abuse problems.

Seeking Safety was the focus of a study of sleep disturbances in male and female victims of a recent crime who met the criteria for PTSD (Germain, et al., 2007). During 90-minute treatment sessions, participants received psychoeducation about nightmares, imagery practice with rescripting, and control and maintenance of stimuli. The results showed a marked decrease in dream frequency, an improvement in daytime PTSD symptoms, a small to moderate improvement in sleep quality and disturbance, and no change in symptoms of anxiety and depression. While the results are promising, they are preliminary. Further research on Seeking Safety with larger samples is recommended.

In a study of 24 participants with recent trauma due to assaults, car accidents, and one who witness a murder, Lee, et al. (2002) conducted a study with use of Stress Inoculation Training with Prolonged Exposure (SITPE) and EMDR. Most participants had prior mental health problems. Participants were provided one of the modalities by random selection. Assessment instruments were completed at the initial session, post-treatment and three months follow-up to treatment. The portion of the study utilizing SITPE is of value to this population. This modality manual was firmly adhered to and seven sessions were provided. Six sessions included engagement, education, and coping skills with one session of prolonged exposure. The results of this study showed clinical significant change for both modalities. Of those who were treated with SITPE, 75 percent no longer met the criteria for PTSD followed by 83 percent at the three-month treatment follow-up. Yet there were some statistically significant differences with regards to symptoms and distress finding those who were treated with SITPE did not meet the criteria for clinically significant improvement or a reduction in intrusion symptoms as quickly as those who received EMDR. It was recommended to increase the number of session of SITPE for greater efficacy.

Survivors of extreme natural disasters

Natural disasters can not only evoke extreme terror, but can also devastate homes, places of employment, and cause financial ruin. Hurricanes, tsunamis, tornadoes, and floods happen worldwide, and have killed and wounded millions of people. As we will discuss in the next chapter, often those who provide services to victims of natural disasters live in the same region as those they serve and may be impacted themselves by the event. External aid is essential when these disasters strike, but there can be concern regarding lack of understanding of culture and norms of the affected region.

Following the massive destruction from Hurricane Katrina in 2005 that devastated many states along the Gulf Coast in the US, Madrid and Grant (2008) identified safety needs as the primary concern of victims, followed by family reunification, community connectedness, cultural competence in workers, and normalization of routine.

Narrative Exposure Therapy (NET) utilizes the tradition components of Narrative Therapy but rather than processing the experience of the trauma by only utilizing narrative techniques, NET theorizes that autobiographic memories related to trauma are "shattered," fragmented, and incomplete. The goal of NET is to reconstruct these memories so that they make sense and become part of a past experience (Bichescu, et al., 2007). Zang, et al. (2013) conducted a randomized control study of the use of NET for 22 trauma survivors of the Sichuan earthquake in China. The participants met the criteria for PTSD. Those who were in the treatment group compared to a wait-list had significant reductions in PTSD symptoms and an increase in posttraumatic growth after participating in NET.

In 1999, Turkey experienced a massive earthquake that crippled the populated coastal area of Marmar. Twenty-five thousand people were killed and more than 750,000 people were left homeless. Recognizing the emotional trauma of the many survivors, the Turkish Psychological Association established mental health clinics in seven tent cities providing pro bono services. This research study provided EMDR to 58 participants who met the criteria of PTSD and were free of symptoms of psychosis and suicidal/homicidal thoughts or plans (Konuk, et al., 2006). Participants provided pre and post (eight sessions) treatment data via selected instruments. The PTSD Symptom Scale Self Report (PSS-SR) provided clinically significant data supporting the use of EMDR for victims of natural disasters. With an average of approximately five sessions, the positive outcomes were maintained over time. It was also noted that the levels of education among the participants was inversely proportionate to the degree of symptoms experienced post treatment; lesser the education the greater the reporting of symptom intensity.

While the literature mostly captures the inclusion of spirituality in a Western approach to trauma recovery, there is little written on the use of spirituality by those in countries with little or no resources to provide options for recovery. However, according to Fernando and Hebert (2011) capitalizing on spiritual beliefs may contribute to resilience following a natural disaster. In survivors of the Sri Lanka tsunami and Hurricane Katrina there was commonality in core elements of resiliency among interviewed female survivors of both disasters (Fernando and Hebert, 2001). The use of faith and the practice of one's religion was cited as a source of support and the most meaningful resources by survivors of the Sri Lanka tsunami and Hurricane Katrina. Both groups reported that reliance on their faith, prayer, and hope was of greatest importance in their recovery.

In a study utilizing the manualized Trauma Recovery and Empowerment Model (TREM), therapists who were also versed in theology and trauma recovery treated women over the age of 55 who had survived at least one traumatic event, as either a child or an adult, and had a history of a Christian tradition. The intent was to learn of the effectiveness of a group treatment program that was focused upon one's spirituality. Utilizing group sessions, the participants were randomly selected to be part of a control group of 22 members or in the experimental or treatment group of 21 members. The group sessions included discussions on spiritual histories, gifts, recovery planning, spiritual solutions to recovery barriers, and strategies to maintaining one's recovery. Pre-treatment, post-treatment, and follow-up (three months) assessments were conducted on all participants who completed the group sessions. Results showed statistical and clinical significance of evidence linking spiritual treatment interventions and the reduction in trauma symptoms (Bowland, *et al.*, 2012).

An emerging treatment model utilized in Kenya, Rwanda, China, Haiti, and the US is the Trauma Resiliency Model (TRM). TRM is a biologically based model that approaches treatment from the perspective that the mind and body are not separate entities, but interdependent (Leitch and Miller-Karas, 2009). From this perspective, talk-therapy that focuses only on cognition may be helpful, but incomplete in treating trauma survivors. Without addressing the fear circuitry, and stress dysregulation that may occur following trauma, attempts to engage the prefrontal cortex may prove inadequate. Following the 2008 massive earthquake that hit the Sichuan province in China, training on TRM was provided to 350 doctors, nurses, and counselors over an 18-month period. Scaling instruments were utilized to assess the perceived applicability of the information received. The response was a 97 percent positive rating that the training was between "moderately and very useful" in their work with post-earthquake survivors.

In summary, while trauma experienced solely in adulthood may not have the same impact neurobiologically as it does in childhood, there are indications of similar recovery issues related to safety, cognition, and emotion regulation. Interventions that target related symptoms appear to provide sustainable reduction in distress. These findings are encouraging and should foster expansion of these sorts of applications.

Chapter 9

Understanding compassion fatigue

The content of this book relates to the impact of trauma across populations and provides information on the detrimental effects of chronic trauma exposure. Those who provide services to trauma survivors are also exposed to trauma, either by listening to the stories of trauma survivors or by being in at-risk settings while providing services. Professionals who work in the area of trauma can experience symptoms that begin to mirror trauma clients. Through the years, this phenomenon has been called several things: burnout, vicarious trauma (McCann and Pearlman, 1990), secondary traumatic stress (STS) (Bride and Figley, 2009), and compassion fatigue (Figley, 1995). Compassion fatigue (CF) is not the same as the psychodynamic concept of countertransference whereby the practitioner over-identifies with the client in order to satisfy unmet needs. Compassion fatigue is exhaustion from long-term emotionally demanding situations (Figley, 2002). CF is found primarily in clinical settings (Adams, *et al.*, 2006). Within the chapter, we present the warning signs of CF, many of which are subtle. We will also demonstrate how CF or STS can affect professionals in their personal and professional lives. Finally, we offer efficacious strategies for self-care and prevention of CF.

Warning signs of compassion fatigue

Most trauma practitioners enter their field with passion and compassion related to the suffering of others. While essential in direct practice, professionals who experience compassion overload can develop detrimental symptoms that can be serious and life altering. Compassion fatigue diminishes empathy. Empathic engagement with trauma survivors often involves re-experiencing the trauma experience through the voice of the client. When CF occurs, practitioners may identify avoidance behaviors and increased emotional arousal related to their work with trauma survivors (Adams, *et al.*, 2006).

Poor self-care, past unresolved trauma, inability to control work stressors, and absence of work satisfaction have been identified as contributors to developing CF symptoms (Figley, 1995). Working with clients who have experienced trauma can impair professional caregivers in cognitive, emotional, and behavioral domains (Figley, 1995, 2002). Table 9.1 provides an overview of some of the warning signs of CF.

Table 9.1 Warning signs of compassion fatigue

Cognitive	Emotional	Behavioral
Difficulty concentrating	Increased anxiety	Withdrawn
Diminished self-esteem	Emotional numbness	Impatient
Apathy	Anger	Sleep disturbances
Fixation on trauma	Feelings of helplessness	Change in appetite
Feelings of self-doubt	Depression	Use of smoking, alcohol, other substances for coping
Trauma imagery	Feeling overwhelmed	Hypervigilance

Source: adapted from Figley, 1995, 2002.

As noted in Table 9.1, symptoms of CF can cause considerable distress, many of which mirror the distress observed in trauma survivors. Physical manifestations of these symptoms can develop in addition to the emotional and cognitive symptoms, and contribute to distress. Just as trauma survivors can experience disruption in social and occupational functioning, so can practitioners who work with this population.

Personal and professional consequences of compassion fatigue

In a meta-analysis of occupational trauma found in humanitarian relief workers (Connorton, *et al.*, 2012), the five most common occupational traumas identified were:

- frightening situations (55–78 percent)
- threats or being chased (16–47 percent)
- forced separation from family (40 percent)
- shelling or bombing of office or home (13–43 percent)
- hostility of the local population (10–37 percent).

Additionally, humanitarian relief workers experienced secondary trauma through witnessing, or having knowledge of trauma experiences in the local populations where they were working.

There is a cost to empathy. In a Canadian nursing study on compassion fatigue (Austin, *et al.*, 2009), nurses identified ways that they had begun to shield themselves from the suffering of their patients. They reported feelings of irritability and negativity that were not only present in their work setting, but were also carried into their personal lives. In a similar study on compassion fatigue, Neville and Cole (2013) identified an increase in fatigue levels in 196 nurse participants when compared to an earlier study. This was attributed to increased complexity in care, higher demands placed on nurses, and an emphasis on cost containment.

Many professionals are regularly exposed to violence in their work settings. This repeated exposure may also place these professional at risk for secondary trauma (Versola-Russo, 2006). In a study of 206 social workers who were directly involved in counseling clients affected by the September 11, 2011 attacks on the World Trade Center, Adams, *et al.* (2006) identified unsupportive work environments to be associated with job burnout. Job burnout was statistically significant in its relation to psychological distress. Work environments can contribute to negative CF outcomes. By examining the predictive ability of empathy, emotional separation, occupational stress, and social support on STS, a study of 121 hospital social workers revealed that emotional separation and occupational stress were the strongest predictors of secondary traumatic stress (Badger, *et al.*, 2008).

The occupational setting plays an important role in contributing to, or mitigating the effects of, compassion fatigue. A study of 154 social workers who work directly with family violence or sexual assault revealed that those who felt supported by their work environment, supervisors, and co-workers demonstrated lower levels of STS (Choi, G., 2011). In a sample of 764 emergency workers, compassion satisfaction was positively correlated with efficacy beliefs, Sense of Community, and the use of active coping strategies. Conversely, burnout and CF were correlated with dysfunctional coping strategies such as distraction and self-criticism (Cicognani, *et al.*, 2009).

Trauma practitioners and self-care

The ability for a practitioner to regulate their emotional response to their client's pain may contribute, or mitigate, personal distress in their professional life (Thomas, 2013). Findings from a study of 171 clinical social workers indicate that the inability to keep perspective related to the pain of others and manage emotional reactions may contribute to CF more than empathy overload. Methods for this self-management may be intrinsic to some, and learned by others. Self-management may be dependent on personality traits. External locus and low optimism may be risk factors for developing CF (Injeyan, *et al.*, 2011).

Radey and Figley (2007) identified factors that contribute to what they call "compassion satisfaction." According to Radey and Figley, physical, intellectual, and social resources are contributing factors that promote well-being in practitioners. Self-care in the form of balance between work and personal life is also identified as contributing to compassion satisfaction. Maturity and length of time in practice also appears to contribute to compassion satisfaction (Craig and Sprang, 2010).

Strong human relationships are also an important component of self-care and appear to mitigate the impact of compassion fatigue. One of the most cited personal resources noted by practitioners who work with trauma survivors is social support. In a study of 196 nurses, findings revealed that spiritual growth and interpersonal relationships directly correlated to health promotion and compassion satisfaction (Neville and Cole, 2013). Following the September 11, 2001 attacks on the World Trade Center in New York City, clinical social workers provided approximately 50 percent of the crisis counseling offered. In a study of 481 of these social workers (Tosone, *et al.*, 2011), attachment styles were directly associated with resilience. Those less securely attached demonstrated higher rates of trauma-related stress.

In a study of 276 occupational health workers, human resource staff, counselors, and police family liaisons, Tehrani (2009) determined that over 70 percent of the participants drew upon friends and colleagues for support. Exercise, prayer, and healthy eating were also cited as self-care strategies. Alkema, *et al.* (2008) evaluated the relationship between self-care, compassion fatigue, burnout, and compassion satisfaction among 37 hospice care providers. Using self-report measures, study subjects were asked to complete rating scales relative to the study variables. The findings revealed that as compassion fatigue increased, self-activities decreased. These findings were similar in respect to burnout and self-care. Compassion satisfaction correlated with emotional, spiritual, and balance subscales, but not physical, psychological, or workplace subscales. These findings may underscore the role that emotional and spiritual self-care, and workplace-professional balance play in mitigating the potential of developing compassion fatigue. Additionally, scores related to self-care appear to have broad application; those who practiced self-care in one area appear to be more prone to practice self-care in other areas of their life.

An interesting finding in a study of 532 trauma specialists related to compassion satisfaction, burnout, and compassion fatigue was the use of evidence-based practice and its correlation to compassion satisfaction (Craig and Sprang, 2010). Along with age and years of experience, the use of evidence-based practice was statistically significant in decreasing CF and burnout and increasing compassion satisfaction.

There are many ways to combat compassion fatigue and it is important that each practitioner practice self-awareness and find methods of prevention that best fit their own lifestyle and value system. When you review the warning signs of CF identified in Table. 9.1 it is evident that many of the symptoms we see in clients can now be applied to professionals who work with trauma survivors. These symptoms can be serious, cause marked distress in a professional's personal life, and impair occupational functioning. In Table 9.2, we present a few suggestions that may be helpful in combatting CF.

Table 9.2 Self-care strategies to combat compassion fatigue

Strategy	Rationale
Incorporate any exercise or activity that utilizes large muscle groups (walking, running, biking, etc.)	Stress-induced neurochemicals are biologically engineered for movement. Exercise activates muscles and improves oxygenation.
Practice grounding behaviors	Increased stress can interfere with the hippocampal function of context. Reminders of your own safety, family, and life pleasures can foster perspective and disengagement from others' trauma.
Practice self-awareness	Take changes in mood, motivation, pleasure, and use of substances (including food) seriously.
Utilize support	Isolation is a warning sign of CF and support has been identified as a major buffer that mitigates distress. Create, foster, or utilize existing support systems.
Set boundaries	Setting healthy limits is essential in all human relationships, including professional settings. Identify areas where boundaries are diffuse and work to set clear limits on your time and resources.
Plan time for yourself	Self-care is essential to health and requires time allocation and planning. Identify activities that bring you pleasure and promote a sense of well-being. These can be hobbies, spiritual practices, family activities, or intellectual pursuits. While our clients are important, at the end of our life, they will not be there.

As noted in earlier discussion in this chapter, social support appears to be a strong protective factor in mitigating CF. We also encourage administrators in trauma-related practice settings to invest in supportive procedures that incorporate organizational support for practitioners who work with trauma survivors. Education and training on trauma and self-care, at a minimum, would be an investment in the future of trauma practitioners. A trauma-informed organization should incorporate the principles that have been identified as beneficial to clients to ensure that the practitioners also benefit.

Chapter 10

Future directions in trauma-informed care

The intent of this book was to provide an understanding of how research from the field of neuroscience related to psychological trauma can influence direct practice with survivors of trauma. The application of neuroscience knowledge to direct practice has some intrinsic barriers; access to research is often limited and the process of obtaining, and translating, scientific findings into language that mental health providers can understand, is labor intensive. The research focus of this book was to provide a condensed overview of trauma across populations, and to incorporate relevant neuroscience information with related treatment options. In this chapter, we summarize our findings, provide data on trends in trauma-informed care, cultural considerations for portability of treatment, and present a rubric for determining treatment choices.

There are numerous governmental, and non-governmental, entities that promote trauma-informed care in settings for the homeless, victims of crime, mental health clients, and child-welfare agencies (NCDVTMH, 2012; NCSTN, n.d.; NCTIC, n.d.; US Department of Health and Human Services, n.d.). Many of these agencies provide solid principles that should assist in the creation of trauma-informed service organizations. Creating a trauma-informed milieu is not an easy task, no matter how clearly defined the guidelines are. Despite efforts by policy makers in the UK, many mental health services do not demonstrate a trauma informed approach to care (Rose, *et al.*, 2012). Bloom (2007) states that organizations that work with troubled clients face enormous stress–related issues with funding, regulatory pressures, and political environments; over time, these high-stress organizations can become punitive toward clients, hierarchal, and coercive. In order for organizations to develop a trauma-informed culture, they must understand the current paradigms that exist within their organizations. According to Harris and Fallot (2001), trauma-informed care does not necessarily mean that an agency provides trauma treatment. Instead, a trauma-informed approach to services creates an environment where clients feel safe and welcomed. They argue that agencies see trauma survivors regularly, but unless trauma treatment is a focus of the client's visit, clients are rarely asked about their trauma history. Additionally, trauma-informed means that we understand the far-reaching impact trauma has on behavior, cognition, and emotion, but within the context of the whole person. Trauma-informed means that we treat people, not only symptoms.

As we have discussed throughout this book, the neurobiological underpinnings of trauma-related mental dysfunction begins within the fear circuitry in the brain. When over-activated on a continuous basis, the initial purpose of this system, safety, can become distorted and contribute to anxiety, depression, cognitive alterations, and impulsivity (Foa and Kozak, 1986; Perry, 2006). In both children and adults, supportive relationships appear to help mitigate the overactive fear system (Stalker, et al., 2005; Radan, 2007), but relationships can also suffer as a result of trauma.

Normal procedures in service delivery settings can feel threatening to trauma survivors, cause them to feel unsafe, and trigger trauma cues (Elliot, et al., 2005). How they are treated when they enter a service agency, the tone of voice of a receptionist, or the questions they are asked can cause fear and anxiety, both of which contribute to clients refusing to return for assistance. There is evidence of some progress in changing service delivery in relation to trauma-informed care. In a recent study in the US, 66 percent of over 10,000 substance-abuse treatment centers reported that they included trauma-related interventions in their agencies (Capezza and Najavits, 2012).

Children in "care" are the clients unquestionably most vulnerable to re-traumatization by a system designed to protect them. Sexual abuse, physical abuse, neglect, and family violence are the reasons children find themselves in the custody of government-run agencies and child-welfare systems. These systems include courts, child-welfare agencies, and mental health agencies, and many children are placed in multiple foster-care settings and frequently have to change schools and lose their peer groups (Hummer, et al., 2010). Except in very rare circumstances, all of the personnel in this system are strangers to these children. Despite the good intentions of child welfare, this process can result in "system generated trauma" that can be equally damaging to a child (Ryan, et al., 2006). Any residential setting where a child is placed following a traumatic event should provide a place of safety from the child's perspective (Bloom, et al., 2003).

In a study of Florida's out-of-home mental health treatment programs for children, Hummer, *et al.* (2010) evaluated the degree that trauma-informed care was being implemented in three statewide inpatient psychiatric programs (SIPP), two therapeutic group care (TGC) settings, and two therapeutic foster care (TFC) homes that had been identified as already using trauma-informed approaches to care. Their findings revealed inconsistencies especially in regard to power; generally, power resided in the hands of the staff, and while three facilities had activities, such as "house council" that included input from the youth, the researchers could not determine if there was any change as a result of the input from administrators. Additionally, while all settings identified mechanisms to prepare children for transitions into other settings, they noted that external uncertainties and the unpredictable nature of placement availability made this difficult. From a neurobiological perspective, these findings are problematic. Feeling safe occurs with a certain degree of predictability and sense of control. In children, the sense of control is often obtained by trust in adult caregivers, and the feeling that caregivers are looking out for the child's best interest.

According to Perry and Hambrick (2008), attempts to create therapeutic treatment settings for children who have experienced trauma are poorly conceptualized and unrealistic without a clear understanding of the basic principles of brain development. Research from the Child Trauma Academy (Perry, 2006; Perry and Hambrick, 2008) promotes moving from a purely medical model of treatment to neurobiological and developmentally sensitive models of treating child trauma survivors. This approach has been coined the Neurosequential Model of Therapeutics (NMT). Early childhood adversity can result in a child remaining in a persistent state of fear because primitive reactions to threat, over time, become entrenched in the developing brain. According to the NMT approach, assessment of fear and adaptive reactions from a developmental perspective is fundamental in treating trauma in children. A second consideration from the NMT perspective is to assess the impact trauma has had on the child's relationships and vulnerability factors related to resilience. Additional assessment includes issues related to self-regulation and cognitive functioning. According to Perry (2006, 2009), the findings of this assessment should determine the intervention that is developmentally most appropriate for each child.

Approaches to treating the adult population of trauma survivors demonstrate additional inconsistencies in defining and treating trauma. Within the mental health and neuroscience community, existing information related to PTSD is conflicting. Following a traumatic event, many people experience emotional numbing, dissociation, sleep difficulties, avoidance behaviors, and hypervigilance. However, 75 to 90 percent of trauma survivors do not go on to develop PTSD (Sadock and Sadock, 2007). Future research is needed to help us understand the variances in responses to trauma among survivors. The age-old nature vs. nurture question lingers regarding resilience to trauma.

In an attempt to determine if there were bio-behavioral markers of PTSD, Zoladz and Diamond (2013) conducted a comprehensive review of existing PTSD research. Their findings indicate that genetic/epigenetic factors may provide promising indicators of PTSD risk factors. There is strong evidence of increased amygdala activity during fear conditioning, and PTSD symptoms may provide a reliable bio-behavioral marker, as does reduced prefrontal cortex (PFC) size and function indicate a bio-behavioral marker. The question remains regarding the possibility of pre-existing conditions related to volumes in the hippocampus, the amygdala, and the prefrontal cortex or whether these anomalies are results of prolonged exposure to trauma. Animal studies indicate that chronic stress suppresses PFC synaptic plasticity. Reduced PFC functioning contributes to inadequate fear extinction, reduced executive functioning, and memory consolidation. Chronic stress adversely affects hippocampal plasticity and memory. Zoladz and Diamond summarize their research findings by noting that lack of consensus on many aspects of PTSD suggests that different subtypes of PTSD have different biological profiles. The complex interplay between developmental, genetic, endocrine, and neurobiological irregularities found in persons with PTSD indicate that a simplistic diagnostic view of this disorder may need to be re-examined.

Culture and trauma-informed care

The global issue of trauma and the variances of available resources offer us the opportunity to explore how we may better offer trauma-recovery services that are cost-efficient and realistic across cultures. If developing trauma-informed practice standards is primarily to broaden our understanding of challenging behaviors and emotions of trauma survivors, it stands to reason that adding further pathology to the issue only serves to compound the problem. Understanding "normal" responses to trauma helps move us away from seeing trauma from a pathology perspective and move toward a more holistic approach to healing.

The word trauma is rooted in the ancient Greek language meaning "wound." If we understand trauma, we know that wounds hurt, and can leave scars. This is also true with psychological trauma. Our struggle is to find methods that foster healing and minimize scarring. This should be the primary goal of any intervention. Many of the treatment modalities identified in this book as trauma-informed have very sophisticated guidelines and treatment protocols. However, it is important to recognize the high level of education and skill that proponents of these treatment methods rely upon. In the research and practice models we reviewed, those who delivered treatment were referred to as practitioners, clinicians, therapists, or psychotherapists. This outlook on specialization is widespread in many so-called "Western" countries. In the US, most state laws prohibit providing independent "psychotherapy" services without at least a master's degree and a clinical license. The motivation behind legislative mandates in professional regulation is an attempt to protect vulnerable members of the public from people who, without proper training, can cause serious harm. We have no quarrel with that intent. However, a broader understanding of trauma-informed care may mean we need to take a step back and look at this issue from a broader perspective. None of the research reviewed used the term *practitioner*; we made that adjustment in the narrative of this text to keep from stumbling over discipline-specific language and losing the intent of the treatment. Without the help of psychiatrists, psychologists, social workers, and counselors, people all over the world recover from trauma. In the remotest regions of the hinterlands, trauma occurs, and in those same regions, people heal, how?

While this is a very important question, we do not have the answer to it. The lack of research from non-Western cultures inhibits our understanding of what we would consider "alternative" methods for healing. This puts us in danger of ethnocentric approaches to care. A search for alternative methods to help people recover from catastrophic events should be an ongoing quest and in no way denigrates the current, highly effective, treatment methods that help provide significant relief from the destructive, and distressing, symptoms of trauma. However, Miller (2007) recommends that twenty-first century trauma psychology should include perspectives that bridge similarities and differences among countries and cultures.

When we explore current trauma-informed treatment approaches, it is likely that some of the *constructs* that contribute to success may occur in numerous other settings. The feeling of safety, conceptualized in a variety of culturally specific ways, would have the same neurobiological effect as one would get from formal treatment. The brain is not interested in the method, only the result. Broadening our understanding of the neurobiological underpinnings that may explain successful treatment can help us begin to move away from a narrow pathology-based view of trauma and assist to broaden concepts to other regions and populations.

A powerful example of a culturally specific trauma perspective is demonstrated in a study of female survivors of the No Gun Ri massacre during the Korean War (Choi, S., 2011). In the early stages of the Korean War, hundreds of unarmed civilian refugees huddled under the railroad bridge near the village of No Gun Ri and were killed by American troops. Until the early 1990s, the South Korean government prohibited any stories that implicated US or South Korean troops in the killing of civilians. By collecting oral history from survivors, Choi noted that these women began to feel empowered to retell their own story, thus shifting their relationship with the story to a historical perspective. Within the constructs of Confucian ideas of motherhood, three types of stories emerged, the dedicated mother, the disappeared mother, and the survived mother. This contrasts with hero-oriented patriarchal views of war that dominate the existing South Korean culture and lend voice to the women's individual trauma stories. At first glance, there are components of this process that are comparable to Narrative Therapy, but there is a dearth in this sort of comparative research.

One of the challenges of comparative research is lack of consensus on definitions and meanings of events, development, and rights across cultures. In a cross-cultural study of children's perspectives on self-determination and their rights, Cherney and Shing (2008) examined the responses of 12-year-olds from a collectivistic culture (Chinese-Malaysian), an individualistic culture (the United States), and a Western European culture (Switzerland). While most of their findings appeared to be culture-normed, they found some universal findings; most notably that the majority of the 100 children surveyed felt personal autonomy and human rights were basic rights. This perspective did not appear to be influenced by culture. Findings such as these help us understand commonalities that exist across cultures. These commonalities can help provide a foundation for cultural portability. It may very well be that data obtained from the social sciences provide valuable insight into treatment development from a cross-cultural perspective.

F.E.A.R.: A rubric to understand trauma

Our research on how neuroscience influences practice has identified some recurring themes that arise from both the neuroscience literature and the treatment literature. In bodies of research from these two fields, residual symptoms, in both children and adults, related to trauma exposure fall into four distinct areas: difficulty in obtaining a state of calm (fear extinction); controlling emotions; attentional bias and cognitive distortions; and long-term relational issues. These areas of posttrauma dysfunction, we believe, should provide a foundation for understanding the types of symptoms that, from a neurobiological perspective, can be expected when working with survivors of trauma. Ironically, the acronym for fear extinction, emotion regulation, attentional bias and cognitive distortions, and relational issues is F.E.A.R. Figure 10.1 provides a diagram of the F.E.A.R. rubric.

Each of the components of F.E.A.R. describe specific functions of the brain may be at risk for adaptive dysfunction after trauma. We say adaptive dysfunction because under normal stress conditions, these same systems would not only be useful, they would be lifesaving. However, as we have already discussed, overuse of this fear-response system creates neurobiological adaptations that cause long-term distress in human functioning. We would encourage the use of F.E.A.R. as a rubric for understanding trauma symptoms and for choosing an intervention; F.E.A.R. is not a treatment model. F.E.A.R. offers an easily remembered mnemonic to understand why clients with a trauma history may behave the way they do. Table 10.1 provides examples of relative neuroscience research related to the F.E.A.R. domains.

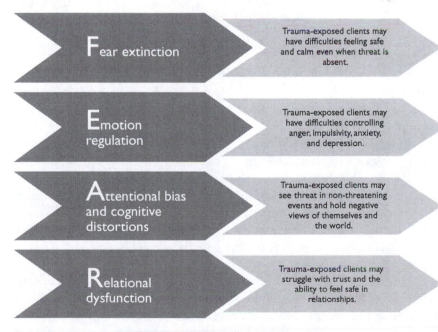

Figure 10.1 F.E.A.R.: A rubric for understanding trauma

Table 10.1 The neuroscience behind F.E.A.R.

Fear extinction	Rogan, *et al.*, 1997; Derryberry and Reed, 2002; Pine and Cohen, 2002; Izutsu, *et al.*, 2004; Corcoran, 2005; Anda, *et al.*, 2006; Perry, 2006; Briere, *et al.*, 2008; Grillon, 2008; Liston, *et al.*, 2009; Rodrigues, *et al.*, 2009; Graham and Milad, 2011; Juster, *et al.*, 2011; Kim, *et al.*, 2011; Sehlmeyer, *et al.*, 2011; Linnman, *et al.*, 2012; McEwen, *et al.*, 2012
Emotion regulation	Dias, *et al.*, 1996; Rogan, *et al.*, 1997; Brown, *et al.*, 1999; Pine and Cohen, 2002; Haller and Miles, 2004; Izutsu, *et al.*, 2004; Anda, *et al.*, 2006; Luecken, *et al.*, 2006; Perry; 2006; Banks, *et al.*, 2007; Briere and Rickards, 2007; Briere, *et al.*, 2008; Goldin, *et al.*, 2009; Liston, *et al.*, 2009; Rodrigues, *et al.*, 2009; Rao, *et al.*, 2010; Graham and Milad, 2011; Juster, *et al.*, 2011; Kim, *et al.*, 2011; McEwen, *et al.*, 2012; Nickerson, *et al.*, 2012
Attentional bias and cognitive distortions	Dias, *et al.*, 1996; Pine and Cohen, 2002; Branscombe, *et al.*, 2003; Haller and Miles, 2004; Izutsu, *et al.*, 2004; Anda, *et al.*, 2006; Luecken, *et al.*, 2006; Perry, 2006; Bar-Haim, *et al.*, 2007; Briere and Rickards, 2007; Briere, *et al.*, 2008; Cisler, *et al.*, 2009; Goldin, *et al.*, 2009; Liston, McEwen, and Casey, 2009; Rodrigues, *et al.*, 2009; Hayes, *et al.*, 2010; El Khoury-Malhame, *et al.*, 2011; Hedges and Woon, 2011; Juster, *et al.*, 2011; McEwen, *et al.*, 2012; Blair, *et al.*, 2013
Relational problems	Roche, *et al.*; 1999; Muller, *et al.*, 2000; Pine and Cohen, 2002; Haller and Miles, 2004; Anda, *et al.*, 2006; Luecken, *et al.*, 2006; Perry; 2006; Alexander, 2009; Briere and Rickards, 2007; Briere, *et al.*, 2008; Pierrehumbert, *et al.*, 2010; Juster, *et al.*, 2011

Each of the domains of F.E.A.R. has been identified as problematic in all of the populations discussed in this text. Any trauma survivor who exhibits posttrauma adverse symptoms may struggle with regulation in these domains. However, those who experienced trauma during important developmental stages in childhood may experience more challenges in recovery than those who experienced trauma as adults. These populations (children and adult survivors of childhood trauma) were subjected to over-activation of the fear circuitry within the brain during times when important neural connections were being established.

The attempt of this book was to provide an overview of neuroscience research related to trauma and how these findings may be applied to practice with trauma survivors. Trauma–informed care is still an emerging concept. While the concept is becoming normed in the US, it is not clear that the practice of trauma–informed care is by any means universal. There are efforts in that direction, but as we noted earlier, the US model is largely dependent upon specialists trained in mental health.

There may be lessons to learn about trauma recovery away from sophisticated treatment models. Do trauma survivors in remote villages across the world recover from the ill effects of trauma? If so, then how? The answers to these questions are largely unknown due to a gap in research available to examine. While the US models provided here demonstrate hope for trauma survivors, they are time-consuming and costly. If we could better understand why these treatments work, we may be able to develop adaptable interventions. Determining what neural structures improve by intervention should guide future research; and for that work, we will continue to rely on our colleagues in the neuroscience fields.

Further reading

Albright, D. L. and Thyer, B. (2010) Does EMDR reduce Post-Traumatic Stress Disorder symptomatology in combat veterans? *Behavioral Interventions*, 25(1): 1–19.

Bath, H. (2008) The three pillars of trauma-informed care, *Reclaiming Children and Youth*, 17(3): 17–21.

Ben-Ezra, M., Essar, N., and Saar, R. (2005) Post-traumatic reactions among rescue personnel 96 hours after the Hilton Hotel bombing in Sinai: The effect of previous exposure, *Stress and Health: Journal of the International Society for the Investigation of Stress*, 21(4): 269–272.

Benish, S. G., Imel, Z. E., and Wampold, B. E. (2007) The relative efficacy of bona fide psychotherapies for treating post-traumatic stress disorder: A meta-analysis of direct comparisons, *Clinical Psychology Review*, 28(5): 746–758.

Boden, M. T., Kimerling, R., Jacobs-Lentz, J., Bowman, D., Weaver, D., Carney, D., Walser, R., and Trafton, J. A. (2011) Seeking Safety treatment for male veterans with a substance use disorder and post-traumatic stress disorder symptomatology, *Addiction*, 107(3): 578–586.

Bremner, J. D., Soutwick, S. M., Darnell, A., and Charney, D. S. (1996) Chronic PTSD in Vietnam combat veterans: course of illness and substance abuse, *American Journal of Psychiatry*, 153(3): 369–375.

Chaumba, J. and Bride, B. E. (2010) Trauma experiences and Posttraumatic Stress Disorder among women in the United States military, *Social Work in Mental Health*, 8(3): 280–303.

Clark, H. W. and Power, K. A. (2005) Women, co-occurring disorders, and violence study: A case for trauma-informed care, *Journal of Substance Abuse Treatment*, 28(2): 145–146.

Cohen, J. A., Berliner, L., and Mannarino, A. (2010) Trauma focused CBT for children with co-occurring trauma and behavior problems, *Child Abuse and Neglect*, 34(4): 215–224.

Cromer, L. D. and Freyd, J. J. (2009) Hear no evil, see no evil? Associations of gender, trauma history, and values with believing trauma vignettes, *Analyses of Social Issues and Public Policy*, 9(1): 85–96.

D'Andrea, W., Ford, J., Stolbach, B., Pinazzola, J., and van der Kolk, B. A. (2102) Understanding interpersonal trauma in children: Why we need a developmentally appropriate trauma diagnosis, *American Journal of Orthopsychiatry*, 82(2): 187–200.

Davidson, P. R. and Parker, K. C. H. (2001) Eye Movement Desensitization and Reprocessing (EMDR): A meta-analysis, *Journal of Consulting and Clinical Psychology*, 69(2): 306–316.

Flemke, K. (2009) Triggering rage: unresolved trauma in women's lives, *Contemporary Family Therapy: An International Journal*, 31(2): 123–139.

Foa, E. (2009) *Effective Treatments for PTSD*, New York: Guilford Press.

Foa, E. B. and Rauch, S. A. M. (2004) Cognitive changes during prolonged exposure versus prolonged exposure plus cognitive restructuring in female assault survivors with posttraumatic stress disorder, *Journal of Consulting and Clinical Psychology*, 72(5): 879–884.

Friedman, M. (2006) Posttraumatic Stress Disorder among military returnees from Afghanistan and Iraq, *The American Journal of Psychiatry*, 163(4): 586–593.

Gustavsson, A. S. (2011) Costs of disorders of the brain in Europe 2010, *European Neuropsychopharmacology*, 21(10): 718–779.

Jansen, J., Beijers, R., Riksen-Walraven, M., and de Weerth, C. (2010) Cortisol reactivity in young infants, *Psychoneuroendocrinology*, 35(3): 329–338.

Jennings, A. (2004) *Models for Developing Trauma-informed Behavioral Health Systems and Trauma-specific Services*, Alexandria, VA: NASMHPD.

Kaysen, D., Simpson, T., Dillworth, T., Larimer, M., Gutner, C., and Resick, P. (2006) Alcohol problems and Post-Traumatic Stress Disorder in female crime victims, *Journal of Traumatic Stress*, 19(3): 399–403.

Khoo, M. T., Dent, M. T., and Oei, T. P. S. (2011) Group cognitive behavior therapy for military service-related post-traumatic stress disorder: Effectiveness, sustainability, and repeatability, *Australian and New Zealand Journal of Psychiatry*, 45(8): 633–672.

Lieberman, A. F., Chu, A., Van Horn, P., and Harris, W. W. (2011) Trauma in early childhood: Empirical evidence and clinical implications, *Development and Psychopathology*, 23(2): 397–410.

Lindstrom, C. M., Cann, A., Calhoun, L. G., and Tedeschi, R. G. (2013) The relationship of core belief challenge, rumination, disclosure, and sociocultural elements to posttraumatic growth, *Psychological Trauma: Theory, Research, Practice, and Policy*, 5(1): 50–55.

Long, D. and Wong, Y. (2012) Time bound: the timescape of secondary trauma of the surviving teachers of the Wenchuan Earthquake, *American Journal of Orthopsychiatry*, 82(2): 541–250.

Luecken, L., Kraft, A., and Hagan, M. (2009) Negative relationships in the family-of-origin predict attenuated cortisol in emerging adults, *Hormones and Behavior*, 55(3): 412.

Malchiodi, C. (2008) *Creative Interventions with Traumatized Children*, New York: Guilford Press.

Marmion, S. L. and Lundberg-Love, P. (2008) PTSD symptoms in college students exposed to interparental violence: Aare they comparable to those that result from child physical and sexual abuse? *Journal of Aggression, Maltreatment and Trauma*, 17(3): 263–278.

Mirsal, H., Kalyoncu, A., Pektas, O., Tan, D., and Beyazyurek, M. (2004) Childhood trauma in alcoholics, *Alcohol and Alcoholism*, 39(2): 126–129.

Morrissey, J. P., Jackson, E. W., Ellis, A. R., Amaro, H., Brown, V. B., and Najavits, L. M. (2005) Twelve-month outcomes of trauma-informed interventions for women with co-occurring disorders, *Psychiatric Services*, 56(10): 1213–1222.

Najavits, L. M. (2009) Psychotherapies for trauma and substance abuse in women: Review and policy implications, *Trauma, Violence, & Abuse*, 10(3): 290–298.

Najavits, L. M. and Kanukollu, S. (2005) It can be learned, but can it be taught? Results from a state-wide training initiative on PTSD and substance abuse, *Journal of Dual Diagnosis*, 1(4): 41–51.

Najavits, L. M., Ryngala, D., Back, S. E., Bolston, E., Museser, K. T., and Brady, K. T. (2008) Treatment for PTSD and comorbid disorders: A review of the literature, in E. B. Foa, T. M. Keane, M. J. Friedman, and J. Cohen (eds.) *Effective Treatments for PTSD: Practice Guidelines for the International Society for Traumatic Stress Studies*, 2nd edition, New York: Guilford Press.

Naturale, A. (2007) Secondary traumatic stress in social workers responding to disasters: Reports from the field, *Clinical Social Work Journal*, 35(3): 173–181.

Olff, M., Langeland, W., and Gersons, B. P. R. (2005) Effects of appraisal and coping on the neuroendocrine response to extreme stress, *Neuroscience and Biobehavioral Reviews*, 29(3): 457–467.

Peres, J., Mercante, J., and Nasello, A. G. (2005) Psychological dynamics affecting traumatic memories: Implications in psychotherapy, *Psychology and Psychotherapy: Theory, Research and Practice*, 78(4): 431–447.

Perry, B. D. (2002) Childhood experience and the expression of genetic potential: What childhood neglect tells us about nature and nurture, *Brain and Mind*, 3(1): 79–100.

Sapolsky, R. (2005) Sick of poverty, *Scientific American*, 293(6): 92–99.

Shakespeare-Finch, J., Martinek, E., and Tedeschi, R. (2013) A qualitative approach to assessing the validity of the posttraumatic growth inventory, *Journal of Loss and Trauma*, 18(6): 572–579.

Simons, L., Ducette, J., Kirby, K. C., Stahler, G., and Shipley, T. E. (2003) Childhood trauma, avoidance coping, and alcohol and other drug use among women in residential and outpatient treatment programs, *Alcoholism Treatment Quarterly*, 21(4): 37–54.

Sprang, G., Clark, J. J., and Whitt-Woosley, A. (2007) Compassion fatigue, compassion satisfaction, and burnout: Factors impacting a professional's quality of life, *Journal of Loss and Trauma*, 12(3): 259–280.

Sprang, G., Kaak, H. O., Staton-Tindall, M., Clark, J. J., Hubbard, K., Whitt-Woosley, A., Mau, A., Combs, A., and Risk, H. (2009) A response from the field: Perspectives on translating neuroscience to clinical practice, *Journal of Loss and Trauma*, 14(4): 315–346.

Stevens, M. and Higgins, D. J. (2002) The influence of risk and protective factors on burnout experienced by those who work with maltreated children, *Child Abuse Review*, 11(5): 313–331.

Swain, J. E., Lorberbaum, J. P., Kose, S., and Strathearn, L. (2007) Brain basis of early parent–infant interactions: psychology, physiology, and in vivo functional neuroimaging studies, *Journal of Child Psychology and Psychiatry*, 48(3/4): 262–287.

Tarullo, A. R. and Gunnar, M. R. (2006) Child maltreatment and the developing HPA axis, *Hormones and Behavior*, 50(4): 632–639.

Taylor, L. K., Weems, C. F., Costa, N. M., and Carrión, V. G. (2009) Loss and the experience of emotional distress in childhood, *Journal of Loss and Trauma*, 14(1): 1–16.

Tyson, J. (2007) Compassion fatigue in the treatment of combat-related trauma during wartime, *Clinical Social Work Journal*, 35(3): 183–192.

Vernberg, E. M., Steinberg, A. M., Jacobs, A. K., Brymer, M. J., Watson, P. J., Osofsky, J. D., Layne, C. M., Pynoos, R. S., and Ruzek, J. I. (2008) Innovations in disaster mental health: Psychological first aid, *Professional Psychology: Research and Practice*, 39(4): 381–388.

Wall, B. (2008) Healing from war and trauma: Southeast Asians in the U. S.: A Buddhist perspective and the Harvard Program in Refugee Trauma, *Human Architecture: Journal of the Sociology of Self-Knowledge*, VI(3): 105–112.

Whisman, M. A. (2006) Childhood trauma and marital outcomes in adulthood, *Personal Relationships*, 13(4): 375–386.

Widom, C. S., Dutton, M. A., Czaja, S. J., and DuMont, K. A. (2005) Development and validation of a new instrument to assess lifetime trauma and victimization history. *Journal of Traumatic Stress*, 18(5): 519–531.

References

Abou, E. and Goldwaser, G. (2009) Effective psychological treatments for posttraumatic stress disorder: Prolonged exposure therapy, *Research Facilitation*, Naval Center for Combat and Operational Stress Control. Available at: www.med.navy.mil/sites/nmcsd/nccosc/healthProfessionalsV2/reports/Documents/cptAPRFinalVersion.pdf.

Adams, R. E., Boscarino, J. A., and Figley, C. R. (2006) Compassion fatigue and psychological stress among social workers: a validation study, *American Journal of Orthopsychiatry*, 76(1): 103–108.

Adverse Childhood Experiences Study (n.d.) Available from: http://acestudy.org/.

Ainsworth, M. (1989) Attachments beyond infancy, *American Psychologist*, 44(4): 709–716.

Alexander, P. C. (2009) Childhood trauma, attachment, and abuse by multiple partners, *Psychological Trauma: Theory, Research, Practice, and Policy*, 1(1): 78–88.

Alkema, K., Linton, J. M., and Davies, R. (2008) A study of the relationship between self-care, compassion satisfaction, compassion fatigue, and burnout among hospice professionals, *Journal of Social Work in End-of-Life and Palliative Care*, 4(2): 101–119.

Allen, B. and Lauterbach, D. (2007) Personality characteristics of adult survivors of childhood trauma, *Journal of Traumatic Stress*, 20(4): 587–595.

Alvarez, J., McLean, C., Harris, A., Rosen, C., Ruzek, J., and Kimerling, R. (2011) The comparative effectiveness of Cognitive Processing Therapy for male veterans treated in a VHA posttraumatic stress disorder residential rehabilitation program, *Journal of Consulting and Clinical Psychology*, 79(5): 590–599.

Amanao, T., Unal, C. T., and Paré, D. (2010) Synaptic correlates of fear extinction in the amygdala, *Nature Neuroscience*, 13(4): 489–494.

American Psychiatric Association (2000) *Diagnostic and Statistical Manual Of Mental Disorders*, 4th edition, Text Revision (DSM-IV-TR), Washington, DC: American Psychiatric Association.

Anda, R. F., Felitti, V. J., Bremner, D. J., Walker, J. D., Whitfield, C., Perry, B. D., Dube, S. R., and Giles, W. H. (2006) The enduring effects of abuse and related averse experiences in childhood, *European Archives of Psychiatry and Clinical Neurosciences*, 256(3): 174–186, available at: www.theannainstitute.org/ACE%20folder%20for%20website/27TACN.pdf (accessed November 10, 2012).

Anderson, C. L. and Alexander, P. C. (1996) The relationship between attachment and dissociation in adult survivors of incest, *Psychiatry*. 59(3): 240–254.

Antonovsky, A. (1987) *Unraveling the Mystery of Health: How People Manage Stress and Stay Well*, San Francisco: Jossey-Bass.

Atonovsky, A. (1993) The structure and properties of the sense of coherence scale, *Social Science Medicine*, 36(6): 725–733.

Austin, W., Goble, E., Leier, B., and Byrne, P. (2009) Compassion fatigue: The experience of nurses, *Ethics and Social Welfare*, 3(2): 195–214.

Avedisova, A. S. (2011) Psychopharmacotherapy of patients with Post-Traumatic Stress Disorder, *Neuroscience and Behavioral Physiology*, 41(3): 272–276.

Azeem, M. W., Aujla, A., Rammerth, M., Binsfeld, G., and Jones, R. B. (2011) Effectiveness of six core strategies based on trauma-informed care in reducing seclusions and restraints at a child and adolescent psychiatric hospital, *Journal of Child and Adolescent Psychiatric Nursing*, 24(1): 11–15.

Badger, K., Royse, D., and Craig, C. (2008) Hospital social workers and indirect trauma exposure: An exploratory study of contributing factors, *Health and Social Work*, 33(1): 63–71.

Bandura, A. (1982) Self-efficacy mechanism in human agency, *American Psychologist*, 37(2): 122–147.

Bandura, A. (1997) *Self-efficacy: The Exercise of Control*, New York: Freeman.

Banks, S. J., Eddy, K. T., Angstadt, M., Nathan, P. J., and Phan, K. L. (2007) Amygdala-frontal connectivity during emotion regulation, *Social Cognitive and Affective Neuroscience*, 2(4): 303–312.

Bar-Haim, Y., Lamy, D. Pergamin, L. Bakermans-Kranenburg, M. J., and van Ijzendoorn, M. H. (2007) Threat-related attentional bias in anxious and non-anxious individuals: A meta-analytic study, *Psychological Bulletin*, 133(1): 1–24.

Bartholomew, K., and Horowitz, L. M. (1991) Attachment styles among young adults: A test of a four category model, *Journal of Personality and Social Psychology*, 61(2): 226–244.

Bartone, P. T., Eid, J., Johnsen, B. H., Laberg, J. C., and Snook, S. (2009) Big five personality factors, hardiness, and social judgment as predictors of leader performance, *Leadership and Organization Development Journal*, 30(6): 498–521.

Bartone, P., Ursano, R., Wright, K., and Ingraham, L. (1989) The impact of a military air disaster on the health of assistance workers: A prospective study, *The Journal of Nervous and Mental Disease*, 177(6): 317–328.

Beck, A. T. (1991) Cognitive therapy: A 30-year retrospective, *American Psychologist*, 46(4): 368–375.

Beck, A. T. (2008) The evolution of the Cognitive Model of Depression and its neurobiological correlates, *American Journal of Psychiatry*, 165(8): 969–977.

Beck Institute for Cognitive Behavior Therapy (n.d.) Available at: www.beckinstitute.org.

Bichescu, D., Neuner, F., Schauer, M., and Elbert, T. (2007) Narrative exposure therapy for political imprisonment-related chronic posttraumatic stress disorder and depression, *Behavior Research and Therapy*, 45: 2212–2220.

Bird, C. M. and Burgess, N. (2008) The hippocampus and memory: insights from spatial processing, *Nature Reviews Neuroscience*, 9(3): 182–194.

Black, P., Woodworth, M., and Tremblay, M (2012) A review of trauma-informed treatment for adolescents, *Canadian Psychology*, 53(3): 192–203.

Blair, K. S., Vythilingam, M. Crowe, S. L., McCaffrey, D. E., Ng, P., Wu, C. C., Scaramozza, M., Mondillo, K., Pine, D. S., Charney, D. S., and Blair, R. J. R. (2013) Cognitive control of attention is differentially affected in trauma-exposed individuals with and without post-traumatic stress disorder, *Psychological Medicine*, 43(1): 85–95.

Bloom, S. L. (2007) The Sanctuary Model of trauma-informed organizational change, *The Source*, 18(1): 12–17, available at: www.sanctuaryweb.com/PDFs_new/Bloom%20 The%20Sanctuary%20Model%20The%20Source%20Articles%20Sanctuary.pdf.

Bloom, S. L., Bennington-Davis, M., Farragher, B., McCorkle, D., Nice-Martin, K., and Wellbank, K. (2003) Multiple opportunities for creating sanctuary, *Psychiatric Quarterly*, 74(2): 173–190.

Bokore, N. (2009) Female survivors of African wars dealing with the past and present, *Journal of Sociological Research*, 1(1): 1–14.

Bonanno, G. (2004) Loss, trauma, and human resilience, *The American Psychologist*, 59(1): 20–28.

Bonanno, G. A., Rennicke, C., and Dekel, S. (2005) Self-enhancement among high-exposure survivors of the September 11th terrorist attack: Resilience or social maladjustment? *Journal of Personality and Social Psychology*, 88(6): 984–998.

Bonanno, G., Pat-Horenczyk, R., and Noll, J. (2011) Coping flexibility and trauma: The perceived ability to cope with trauma (PACT) Scale, *Psychological Trauma: Theory, Research, Practice, and Policy*, 3(2): 117–129.

Bornstein, R. (2005) Interpersonal dependency in child abuse perpetrators and victims: A meta-analytic review, *Journal of Psychopathology and Behavioral Assessment*, 27(2): 67–76.

Bowland, S., Edmond, T., and Fallot, R. (2012) Evaluation of a spiritually focused intervention with older trauma survivors, *Social Work*, 57(1): 73–82.

Bowlby, J. (1954) The effect of separation from the mother in early life, *The Irish Journal of Medicine*, 29(3): 121–126.

Bowlby, J. (1970) Disruption of affectional bonds and its effects on behavior, *Journal of Contemporary Psychotherapy*, 2(2): 75–86.

Bowlby, J. (1988) *A Secure Base: Parent–Child Attachment and Healthy Hhuman Development*, New York: Basic Books.

Bowlby, J., Ainsworth, M., Boston, M., and Rosenbluth, D. (1956) The effects of mother-child separation: A follow-up study, *British Journal of Medical Psychology*, 29(3/4): 211–247.

Branscombe, N. R., Wohl, M. J. A., Owen, S., Allison, J. A., and N'gbala, A. (2003) Counterfactual thinking, blame assignment, and well-being in rape victims, *Basic and Applied Social Psychology*, 25(4): 265–273.

Bratton, S., Ray, D., Rhine, T., and Jones, L. (2005) The efficacy of play therapy with children: a meta-analytic review of treatment outcomes, *Professional Psychology: Research and Practice*, 36(4): 376–390.

Breed, M., Cilliers, F., and Visser, D. (2006) The factor structure of six Salutogenic constructs, *SA Journal of Industrial Psychology*, 32(1): 74–87.

Bremner, J. D. (2007) Functional neuroimaging in post-traumatic stress disorder, *Expert Review of Neurotherapy*, 7(4): 393–405.

Bremner, J. D., Staib, L. H., Kaloupek, D., Southwich, S. M., Soufer, R., and Charney, D. S. (1999) Neural correlates of exposure to traumatic pictures and sound in Vietnam combat veterans with and without posttraumatic stress disorder: A positron emission study, *Biological Psychiatry*, 45(7): 806–816.

Bride, B. E. (2007) Prevalence of secondary traumatic stress among social workers, *Social Work*, 52(1): 63–70.

Bride, B. and Figley, C. (2009) Secondary trauma and military veteran caregivers, *Smith College Studies in Social Work*, 79(3/4): 314–329.

Briere, J. and Rickards, S. (2007) Self-awareness, affect regulation, and relatedness: differential sequels of childhood versus adult victimization experiences, *The Journal of Nervous and Mental Disease*, 195(6): 497–503.

Briere, J., Kaltman, S., and Green, B. L. (2008) Accumulated childhood trauma and symptom complexity, *Journal of Traumatic Stress*, 21(2): 223–226.

Brown, E. S., Rush, A. J., and McEwen, B. S. (1999) Hippocampal remodeling and damage by corticosteroids: Implications for mood disorders, *Neuropsychopharmacology*, 21(4): 474–484.

Brown, T. H., Mellman, T. A., Alfano, C. A., and Weems, C. F. (2011) Sleep fears, sleep disturbance, and PTSD symptoms in minority youth exposed to hurricane Katrina, *Journal of Traumatic Stress*, 24(5): 575–580.

Bryant, R. A., Creamer, M., O'Donnell, M., Silove, D., and McFarlane, A. C. (2011) Heart rate after trauma and the specificity of fear circuitry disorders, *Psychological Medicine*, 41(12): 2573–2580.

Bush, D. E., Sotres-Bayon, F., and LeDoux, J. E. (2007) Individual differences in fear: Isolating fear reactivity and fear recovery phenotypes, *Journal of Traumatic Stress*, 20(4): 13–22.

Caldwell, B. A. and Redeker, N. (2005) Sleep and trauma: An overview, *Issues in Mental Health Nursing*, 26(7): 721–738.

Campbell, S. and MacQueen, G. (2004) The role of the hippocampus in the pathophysiology of major depression, *Journal of Psychiatric Neuroscience*, 29(6): 417–426.

Capezza, N. M. and Najavits, L. M. (2012) Rates of trauma-informed counseling at substance abuse treatment facilities: reports from over 10,000 programs, *Psychiatric Services*, 63(4): 390–394.

Cardenas, V. A., Samuelson, K. Lenoci, M. Studholme, C., Nyelan, T. C., Marmar, C. R., Schuff, N., and Weiner, M. W. (2011) Changes in brain anatomy during the course of PTSD, *Psychiatry Research: Neuroimaging*, 193(2): 93–100.

Carrión, V. G. and Hull, K. (2010) Treatment manual for trauma-exposed youth: Case studies, *Clinical Child Psychology and Psychiatry*, 15(1): 27–38.

Carrión, V. G., Haas, B. W., Garrett, A., Song, S., and Reiss, A. L. (2010) Reduced hippocampal activity in youth with posttraumatic stress symptoms: An fMRI study, *Journal of Pediatric Psychology. Special Issue: Health Consequences of Child Maltreatment*, 35(5): 559–569.

Carter, R., Aldridge, S., Page, M., and Parker, S. (2009) *The Human Brain Book*, New York: Dorling Kindersley.

CATS Consortium (2007) Implementing CBT for traumatized children and adolescents after September 11: Lessons learned from the Child and Adolescent Trauma Treatments and Services (CATS) Project, *Journal of Clinical Child and Adolescent Psychology*, 36(4): 581–592.

CATS Consortium (2010) Implementation of CBT for youth affected by the World Trade Center disaster: Matching need to treatment intensity and reducing trauma symptoms, *Journal of Traumatic Stress*, 23(6): 699–707.

Chard, K. M., Schumm, J. A., Owens, G. P., and Cottingham, S. M. (2010) A comparison of OEF and OIF veterans and Vietnam veterans receiving Cognitive Reprocessing Therapy, *Journal of Traumatic Stress*, 23(1): 25–32.

Charney, D. S. (2004) Psychobiological mechanisms of resilience and vulnerability: Implications for successful adaptation to extreme stress, *American Journal of Psychiatry*, 161(2): 195–216.

Cherney, I. D. and Shing, Y. L. (2008) Children's nurturance and self-determination rights: A cross-cultural perspective, *Journal of Social Issues*, 64(4): 835–856.

Choi, G. (2011) Organizational impacts on the secondary traumatic stress of social workers assisting family violence or sexual assault survivors, *Administration in Social Work*, 35(3): 225–242.

Choi, S. (2011) Communicating trauma: Female survivors' witnessing the No Gun Ri killings, *Qualitative Inquiry*, 17(1): 23–34.

Christensen, R. C., Hodgkins, C. C., Garces, L., Estlund, K. L., Miller, M. D., and Touchton, R. (2005) Homeless, mentally ill and addicted: A need for abuse and trauma services, *Journal of Health Care for the Poor and Underserved*, 16(4): 615–621.

Chugani, H. T., Behen, M. E., Muzik, O., Juhász, C., Nagy, F., and Chugani, D. C. (2001) Local brain functional activity following early deprivation: A study of postinstitutionalized Romanian orphans, *NeuroImage*, 14(6): 1290–1301.

Cicchetti, D. and Lynch, M. (1995) Failures in the expectable environment and their impact on individual development: The case of child maltreatment, in D. Cicchetti and D. J. Cohen (eds.) *Developmental Psychopathology: Risk, Disorder, and Adaptation, Vol. 2*, New York: Wiley, pp. 32–71.

Cicchetti, D. and Valentino, K. (2006) An ecological transactional perspective on child maltreatment: Failure of the average expectable environment and its influence upon child development, in D. Cicchetti and D. J. Cohen (eds.) *Developmental Psychopathology: Risk, Disorder, and Adaptation, Vol. 3*, 2nd edition, New York: Wiley, pp. 129–201.

Cicognani, E., Pietrantoni, L., Palestini, L., and Prati, G. (2009) Emergency workers' quality of life: The protective role of sense of community, efficacy beliefs and coping strategies, *Social Indicators Research*, 94(3): 449–463.

Cigrang, J., Rauch, S., Avila, L., Bryan, C., Goodie, J., Hryshko-Mullen, A., Peterson, A. L., and Strong Star Consortium (2011) Treatment of active-duty military with PTSD in primary care: Early findings. *Psychological Services*, 8(2): 104–113.

Cisler, J. M., Bacon, A. K., and Williams, N. L. (2009) Phenomenological characteristics of attentional bias towards threat: A critical review, *Cognitive Therapy Research*, 33(2): 221–234.

Clark, L. M. and Hartman, M. (1996) Effects of hardiness and appraisal on the psychological distress and physical health of caregivers to elderly relatives, *Research on Aging*, 18(4): 379–401.

Cloitre, M., Cohen, L. R., Koenen, K. C., and Han, H. (2002) Skills training in affective and interpersonal regulation followed by exposure: A phase-based treatment for PTSD related to childhood abuse, *Journal of Consulting and Clinical Psychology*, 70(5): 1067–1074.

Cloitre, M., Stolbach, B. C., Herman, J. L., van der Kolk, B., Pynoos, R., Wang, J., and Petkova, E. (2009) A developmental approach to complex PTSD: Childhood and adult cumulative trauma as predictors of symptom complexity, *Journal of Traumatic Stress*, 22(5): 399–408.

Cohen, J. A. and Mannarino, A. (1998) Interventions for sexually abused children: Initial treatment outcome findings, *Child Maltreatment*, 3(1): 17–26.

Cohen, J. A. and Mannarino, A. (2004) Treatment of childhood traumatic grief, *Journal of Clinical Child and Adolescent Psychology*, 33(4): 819–831.

Cohen, J. A., Mannarino, A., and Knudsen, K. (2004) Treating childhood traumatic grief: A pilot study, *Journal of the American Academy of Child and Adolescent Psychiatry*, 43(10): 1225–1233.

Cohen, J. A., Mannarino, A. P., Murray, L. K., and Igelman, R. (2006) Psychosocial interventions for maltreated and violence-exposed children, *Journal of Social Issues*, 62(4): 737–766.

Cohen, J. A., Mannarino, A., Kliethermes, M., and Murray, L. (2012) Trauma-focused CBT for youth with complex trauma, *Child Abuse and Neglect*, 36(6): 528–541.

Coifman, K., Bonanno, G., Ray, R., and Gross, J. (2007) Does repressive coping promote resilience? Affective–autonomic response discrepancy during bereavement, *Journal of Personality and Social Psychology*, 92(4): 745–758.

Connorton, E., Perry, M. J., Hemenway, D., and Miller, M. (2012) Humanitarian relief workers and trauma-related mental illness, *Epidemiologic Reviews*, 34(1): 145–155.

Cook, A., Spinazzola, J., Ford, J., Lanktree, C., Blaustein, M., Cloitre, M., DeRosa, R., Hubbard, R., Kagan, R., Liautaud, J., Mallah, K., Olafson, E., and van der Kolk, B. (2005) Complex trauma in children and adolescents, *Psychiatric Annals*, 35(5): 390–398.

Corcoran, K. A. (2005) Hippocampal inactivation disrupts the acquisition and contextual encoding of fear extinction, *Journal of Neuroscience*, 25(39): 8978–8987.

Courtois, C., Ford, J., and Cloitre, M. (2009) Best practices in psychotherapy for adults, in Courtois, C. and Ford, J. (eds.) *Treating Complex Traumatic Stress Disorders An Evidence Based Guide*, New York: The Guildford Press, Chapter 4.

Craig, C. D. and Sprang, G. (2010) Compassion satisfaction, compassion fatigue, and burnout in a national sample of trauma treatment specialists, *Anxiety, Stress, and Coping*, 23(3): 319–339.

Crenshaw, D. A. (2006) An interpersonal neurobiological-informed treatment model for childhood traumatic grief, *Omega: Journal of Death and Dying*, 54(4): 319–335.

Crenshaw, D. A. and Hardy, K. (2007) The crucial role of empathy in breaking the silence of traumatized children in play therapy, *International Journal of Play Therapy*, 12(2): 160–175.

Danese, A. and McEwen, B. S. (2012) Adverse childhood experiences, allostasis, allostatic load, and age-related disease, *Physiology & Behavior*, 106(1): 29–39.

Deblinger, E., Steer, A. R., and Lippmann, J. (1999) Two-year follow-up study of cognitive behavioral therapy for sexually abused children suffering post-traumatic stress symptoms, *Child Abuse and Neglect*, 23(12): 1371–1378.

DeRosa, R. and Pelcovitz, D. (2006) Treating traumatized adolescent mothers: A structured approach, in N. Webb (ed.) *Working with Traumatized Youth in Child Welfare*, New York: Guilford Press.

Derryberry, D. and Reed, M. A. (2002) Anxiety-related attentional biases and their regulation by attentional control, *Journal of Abnormal Psychology*, 111(2): 225–236.

Desai, R. A., Harpaz-Rotem, I., Najavits, L. M., and Rosenheck, R. A. (2008) Impact of the Seeking Safety program on clinical outcomes among homeless female veterans with psychiatric disorders, *Psychiatric Services*, 59(9): 996–1003.

Dhabhar, F. S., Malarkey, W. B., Neri, E., and McEwen, B. S. (2012) Stress induced redistribution of immune cells: From barracks to boulevards to battlefields, a tale of three hormones, *Psychoneuroendocrinology*, 37(9): 1345–1368.

Dias, R., Robbins, T. W., and Roberts, A. C. (1996) Dissociation in the prefrontal cortex of affective and attentional shifts, *Nature*, 380(6596): 69–72.

DiGrande, L., Neria, Y., Brackbill, R. M., Pulliam, P., and Galea, S. (2010) Long-term posttraumatic stress symptoms among 3,271 civilian survivors of the September 11, 2011, terrorist attacks on the World Trade Center, *American Journal of Epidemiology*, 173(3): 291–281.

Dimeff, L. and Linehan, M. M. (2001) Dialectical behavior therapy in a nutshell, *The California Psychologist*, 34: 10–13.

Duke, N., Pettingell, S., McMorris, B., and Borowsky, I. (2010) Adolescent violence perpetration: Associations with multiple types of adverse childhood experiences, *Pediatrics*, 125(4): e778–e786.

Edmond, T., Rubin, A., and Wambach, K. (1999) The effectiveness of EMDR with adult female survivors of childhood sexual abuse, *Social Work Research*, 23(2): 103–116.

Eisenberg, N. and Silver, R (2011) Growing up in the shadow of terrorism youth in America after 9/11, *American Psychologist*, 66(6): 468–481.

Eisold, B. K. (2005) Notes on lifelong resilience: Perceptual and personality factors implicit in the creation of a particular adaptive style, *Psychoanalytic Psychology*, 22(3): 411–425.

El Khoury-Malhame, M., Reynaud, E., Soriano, A., Michael, K., Salgado-Pineda, P., Zendidjian, X., Gellato, C., Eric, F., Lefebvre, M., Rouby, F., Samuelian, J., Anton, J., Blin, O., and Khalfa, S. (2011) Amygdala activity correlates with attentional bias in PTSD, *Neuropsychologia*, 49(7): 1969–1973.

Elliott, D. E., Bjelajac, P., Fallot, R. D., Markoff, L. S., and Reed, B. G. (2005) Trauma-informed or trauma-denied: Principles and implementation of trauma-informed services for women, *Journal of Community Psychology*, 33(4): 461–477.

El Zein, H. L. and Ammar, D. F. (2010) Parent and teacher perceptions of assessing Lebanese children's reaction to war-related stress: A survey of psychological and behavioral functioning, *Journal of Child and Adolescent Trauma*, 3(4): 255–278.

Emanuel, R. (2004) Thalamic fear, *Journal of Child Psychotherapy*, 30(1): 71–87.

Erikson, E. (1963) *Childhood and Society*, New York: W. W. Norton and Co.

Eriksson, M. and Lindström, B. (2005) Validity of Antonovsky's sense of coherence scale: A systematic review, *Journal of Epidemiology and Community Health*, 59(6): 460–466.

Errebo, N., Knipe, J., Forte, K., Karlin, V., and Altayli, B. (2008) EMDR-HAP training in Sir Lanka following the 2004 Tsunami, *Journal of EMDR Practice and Research*, 2(2): 124–139.

Farrell, D., Dworkin, M., Keenana, P., and Spierings, J. (2010) Using EMDR with survivors of sexual abuse perpetrated by Roman Catholic priests, *Journal of EMDR Practice and Research*, 4(3): 124–133.

Felitti, V. and Anda, R. (2009) The relationship of adverse childhood experiences to adult medical disease, psychiatric disorders and sexual behavior: implications for healthcare, in R. Lanius, E. Vermetten, and C. Pain (eds.) *The Impact of Early Life Trauma on Health and Disease The Hidden Epidemic*, New York: Cambridge University Press, pp. 77–87.

Fernando, D. and Hebert, B. (2011) Resiliency and recovery: Lessons from the Asian Tsunami and Hurricane Katrina, *Journal of Multicultural Counseling and Development*, 39(1): 2–13.

Figley, C. R. (1995) *Compassion Fatigue: Coping with Secondary Traumatic Stress Disorder in Those who Treat the Traumatized*, New York/London: Brunner-Routledge Press.

Figley, C. R. (2002) Compassion fatigue: Psychotherapists' chronic lack of self-care, *Journal of Clinical Psychology*, 58(11): 1433–1441.

Foa, E. and Kozak, M. (1986) Emotional processing of fear: exposure to corrective information, *Psychological Bulletin*, 99(1): 20–35.

Foa, E. B., Keane, T. M., Friedman, M. J., and Cohen, J. A. (Eds.) (2009) *Effective Treatments for PTSD Practical Guidelines from the International Society for Traumatic Stress Studies*, 2nd edition, New York. Guilford Press.

Foa, E. B., Rothbaum, B. O., Riggs, D. S., and Murdock, T. B. (1991) Treatment of posttraumatic stress disorder in rape victims: A comparison between cognitive-behavioral procedures and counseling, *Journal of Consulting and Clinical Psychology*, 59(5): 715–723.

Foy, D. W., Glynn, S. M., Ruzek, J. I., and Gusman, F. D. (2002) Trauma focused group therapy for combat-related PTSD, *In Session: Psychotherapy in Practice*, 58(8): 907–918.

Fraser, J. G., Harris-Britt, A., Thakkallapalli, E. L., Kurtz-Costes, B., and Martin, S. (2010) Emotional availability and psychosocial correlates among mothers in substance-abuse treatment and their young infants, *Infant Mental Health Journal*, 31(1): 1–15.

Friborg, D., Hjemdal, O., Martinussen, M., and Rosenvinge, J. (2009) Empirical support for resilience as more than the counterpart and absence of vulnerability and symptoms of mental disorder, *Journal of Individual Differences*, 30(3): 138–151.

Funk, S. (1992) Hardiness: A review of theory and research, *Health Psychology*, 11(5): 335–345.

Furr, J. M., Comer, J. S., Edmunds, J. M., and Kendall, P. C. (2010) Disasters and youth: A meta-analytic examination of posttraumatic stress, *Journal of Consulting and Clinical Psychology*, 78(6): 765–780.

Galea S., Ahren J., Resnick, H., Kilpatrick D., Bucuvalas, M., Gold J., and Vlahov, D. (2002) Psychological sequelae of the September 11 terrorist attacks in New York City, *New England Journal of Medicine*, 346: 982–987.

Gamito, P., Oliveira, J., Rosa, P., Morais, D., Duarte, N., Oliveira, S., and Saraiva, T. (2010) PTSD elderly war veterans: A clinical controlled pilot study, *Cyberpsychology, Behavior, and Social Networking*, 13(1): 43–48.

Ganzel, B., Morris, P., and Wethington, E. (2010) Allostasis and the human brain: integrating models of stress from the social and life sciences, *Psychological Review*, 117(1): 134–174.

Gerardi, M., Rothbaum, B. O., and Astin, M. (2010) Cortisol response following exposure treatment for PTSD in rape victims, *Journal of Aggression, Maltreatment, & Trauma*, 19(4): 349–356.

Germain, A., Richardson, R., Moul, D. E., Mammen, O., Haas, G., Foreman, S. D., Rode, N., Begley, A., and Nofzinger, E. A. (2012) Placebo-controlled comparison of prazosin and cognitive-behavioral treatments for sleep disturbances in US military veterans, *Journal of Psychosomatic Research*, 72(2): 89–96.

Germain, A., Shear, K., Hall, M., and Buysse, D. (2007) Effects of a brief behavioral treatment for PTSD-related sleep disturbances: A pilot study, *Behavior Research and Therapy*, 45(3): 627–632.

Gilbertson, M. W., Shenton, M. E., Ciszewski, A., Kasai, K., Lasko, N. B., Orr, S. P., and Pitman, R. K. (2002) Smaller hippocampal volume predicts pathogenic vulnerability to psychological trauma, *Nature Neuroscience*, 5(11): 1242–1247.

Gilman, R., Schumm, J., and Chard, K. (2012) Hope as a change mechanism in the treatment of posttraumatic stress disorder, *Psychological Trauma: Theory, Research, Practice, and Policy*, 4(3): 270–277.

Gingerich, T. and Leaning, J. (2004) *The Use of Rape as a Weapon of War in the Conflict in Darfur, Sudan*, Program on Humanitarian Crises and Human Rights, François-Xavier Bagnoud Center for Health and Human Rights, Boston, MA: Harvard School of Public Health.

Girdler, S. S., Jamner, L. D., and Shapiro, D. (1997) Hostility, testosterone, and vascular reactivity to stress: Effects of sex, *International Journal of Behavioral Medicine*, 4(3): 242–263.

Goldin, P. R., Manber, T., Hakimi, S., Canli, T., and Gross, J. J. (2009) Neural bases of social anxiety disorder: Emotional reactivity and cognitive regulation during social and physical threat, *Archives of General Psychiatry*, 66(2): 170–180.

Graham, B. M. and Milad, M. R. (2011) The study of fear extinction: implications for anxiety disorders, *The American Journal of Psychiatry*, 168(12): 1255–1265.

Green, D. and Roberts, A. (2008) *Helping Victims of Violent Crime: Assessment, Treatment and Evidence-Based Practice*, New York: Springer Publishing Company.

Grillon, C. (2008) Models and mechanisms of anxiety: Evidence from startle studies, *Psychopharmacology*, 199(3): 421–437.

Gutner, C., Rizvi, S., Monson, C., and Resick, P. (2006) Changes in coping strategies, relationship to the perpetrator, and posttraumatic distress in female crime victims, *Journal of Traumatic Stress*, 19(6): 813–823.

Haller, D. L. and Miles, D. R. (2004) Personality disturbances in drug-dependent women: relationship to childhood abuse, *American Journal of Drug and Alcohol Abuse*, 30(2): 269–286.

Harris, M. F. (2001) *New Directions for Mental Health Services: Using trauma theory to design service systems*, San Francisco, CA: Jossey-Bass.

Harris, M. F. and Fallot, R. D. (2001) Envisioning a trauma-informed service system: A vital paradigm shift, *New Directions for Mental Health Services*, 2001(89): 3–22.

Harvey, M. R. (1996) An ecological view of psychological trauma and trauma recovery, *Journal of Traumatic Stress*, 9(1): 3–23.

Harvey, M. R. (2007) Towards an ecological understanding of resilience in trauma survivors: Implications for theory, research and practice, *Journal of Aggression, Maltreatment, and Trauma*, 14(1/2): 9–32.

Harvey, S. (2008) An initial look at the outcomes for dynamic play therapy, *International Journal of Play Therapy*, 17(2): 86–101.

Harvey, S. A. (1993) Ann: Dynamic play therapy with ritual abuse, in T. Kottman and C. Schaefer (eds.) *Play Therapy in Action: A Case Book for Practitioners*, Northvale, NJ: Aronson, pp. 341–415.

Hayes, J. P., LaBar, K. S., McCarthy, G., Selgrade, E., Nasser, J., Dolcos, F., VISN 6 Mid-Atlantic MIRECC workgroup, and Morey, R. A. (2010) Reduced hippocampal volumes and amygdala activity predicts memory distortions for trauma reminders in combat-related PTSD, *Journal of Psychiatric Research*, 45(5): 660–669.

Hedges, D. W. and Woon, F. L. (2011) Early-life stress and cognitive outcome, *Psychopharmacology*, 214(1): 121–130.

Heim, C. and Nemeroff, C. B. (2001) The role of childhood trauma in the neurobiology of mood and anxiety disorders: Preclinical and clinical studies, *Biological Psychiatry*, 49(12): 1023–1039.

Hensley-Maloney, L. and Varela, R. E. (2009) The influence of hurricane exposure and anxiety sensitivity on panic symptoms, *Child & Youth Care Forum*, 38(3): 135–149.

Herman, J. (1992) Complex PTSD: A syndrome in survivors of prolonged and repeated trauma, *Journal of Traumatic Stress*, 5(3): 377–391.

Hobfoll, S. E., Watson, P., Bell, C. C., Bryant, R. A., Brymer, M. J., Friedman, M. J., Friedman, M., Gersons, B. P., de Jong, J., Layne, C. M., Maguen, S. Neria, Y., Norwood, A. E., Pynoos, R. S., Reissman, D., Ruzek, J. I., Shalev, A. Y., Solomon, Z., Steinberg, A. M., and Ursano, R. J. (2007) Five essential elements of immediate and mid-term mass trauma intervention: Empirical evidence, *Psychiatry*, 70(4): 283–315.

Hofman, S. G. and Smits, J. A. (2008) Cognitive-behavioral therapy for adult anxiety disorders: a meta-analysis of randomized placebo-controlled trials, *Journal of Clinical Psychiatry*, 69(4): 621–632.

Hummer, V. L., Dollard, N., Robst, J., and Armstrong, M. I. (2010) Innovations in implementation of trauma-informed care practices in youth residential treatment: A curriculum for organizational change, *Child Welfare*, 89(2): 79–95.

Iliyasu, Z., Abubakar, I. S., Galadanci, H. S., Hayatu, Z., and Aliyu, M. H. (2013) Prevalence and risk factors for domestic violence among pregnant women in northern Nigeria, *Journal of Interpersonal Violence*, 28(4): 868–883.

Injeyan, M. C., Shuman, C., Shugar, A., Chitayat, D., Atenafu, E. G., and Kaiser, A. (2011) Personality traits associated with genetic counselor compassion fatigue: The roles of dispositional optimism and locus of control, *Journal of Genetic Counseling*, 20(5): 526–540.

Inoue, N. (2009) Evaluation of an EMDR treatment outcome using the Rorschach, the TAT and the IES-R: A case study of a human-caused trauma survivor, *Rorschachiana*, 30(2): 180–218.

Institute of Medicine (2007) *Treatment of Posttraumatic Stress Disorder: An Assessment of the Evidence*, Washington DC: The National Academies Press, available at: http://books.nap.edu/openbook.php?record_id=11955.

Ipser, J. and Stein, D. (2012) Evidence-based pharmacotherapy of post-traumatic stress disorder (PTSD), *The International Journal of Neuropsychopharmacology*, 15(6): 825–840.

Irish, L., Ostrowski, S., Fallon, W., Spoonster, E., Dulmen, M., Sledjeski, E., and Delahanty, D. (2008) Trauma history characteristics and subsequent PTSD symptoms in motor vehicle accident victims, *Journal of Traumatic Stress*, 21(4): 377–384.

Irving, L., Snyder, C. R., Cheavens, J., Gravel, L., Hanke, J., Hilberg, P., and Nelson, P. (2004) The relationships between hope and outcomes at the pretreatment, beginning, and later of psychotherapy, *Journal of Psychotherapy Integration*, 14(4): 419–443.

ISTSS (2013) *Treating Trauma: Cognitive Processing Therapy (CPT)*, available at: www.istss.org/CognitiveProcessingTherapyCPT.htm.

Izutsu, T., Tsutsumi, A., Asukai, N., Kurita, H., and Kawamura, N. (2004) Relationship between a traumatic life event and an alteration in stress response, *Stress and Health: Journal of the International Society for the Investigation of Stress*, 20(2): 65–73.

Jamil, H. and Ventimiglia, M. (2010) Mental health and treatment response among Iraqi refugees as compared to other non-war exposed Arab immigrants: A pilot study in Southeast Michigan, *Journal of Immigrant and Refugee Studies*, 8(4): 431–444.

Juster, R., Bizik, G., Picard, M., Arsenault-Lapierre, G., Sindi, S., Trepanier, L., Marin, M., Wan, N., Sekerovic, Z., Lord, C., Fiocco, A. J., Plusquellec, P., McEwen, B. S., and Lupien, S. J. (2011) A transdisciplinary perspective of chronic stress in relation to psychopathology throughout lifespan development, *Development and Psychopathology*, 23(3): 725–776.

Kaiser Permanente (n.d.). Fast Facts about Kaiser Permanente. Available from: http://share.kaiserpermanente.org/article/fast-facts-about-kaiser-permanente/.

Kandel, E. R. (2000) Disorders of mood: Depression, mania, and anxiety disorders, in E. R. Kandel, J. H. Schwatrz, and T. M. Jessell (eds.) *Principles of Neural Science*, 4th edition, New York: McGraw-Hill.

Kessler, R. C., Sonnega, A., Bromet, E., Hughes, M., and Nelson, C. B. (1995) Posttraumatic stress disorder in the National Comorbidity Survey, *Archives of General Psychiatry*, 52(12): 1048–1060.

Kim, M. J., Loucks, R. A., Palmer, A. L., Brown, A. C., Solomon, K. M., Marchante, A. N., and Whalen, P. J. (2011) The structural and functional connectivity of the amygdala: From normal emotion to pathological anxiety, *Behavioral Brain Research*, 223(2): 403–410.

Kimuna, S. R., Djamba, Y. K., Ciciurkaite, G., and Cherukuri, S. (2013) Domestic violence in India, *Journal of Interpersonal Violence*, 28(4): 773–807.

Kirmayer, L. J., Lemelson, R., and Barad, M. (eds.) (2007) *Understanding Trauma*. Cambridge University Press, Cambridge Books Online, available at: http://dx.DOI.org/10.1017/CBO9780511500008 (accessed May 30, 2013).

Kirmayer, L. J., Narasiah, L., Munoz, M., Rashid, M., Ryder, A. G., Guzder, J., Hassan, G., Rousseau, C., and Pottie, K. (2011) Common mental health problems in immigrants and refugees: general approach in primary care, *Canadian Medical Association Journal*, 183(12): E959–E967.

Klasen, F., Oettingen, G., Daniels, J., and Hubertus, A. (2010) Multiple trauma and mental health in former Ugandan child soldiers, *Journal of Traumatic Stress*, 23(5): 573–591.

Ko, S. J., Kassam-Adams, N., Wilson, C., Ford, J. D., Berkowitz, S. J., Wong, M., Brymer, M. J., and Layne, C. M. (2008) Creating trauma-informed systems: child welfare, education, first responders, health care, juvenile justice, *Professional Psychology, Research and Practice*, 39(4): 396–404.

Kobasa, S C. (1979) Stressful life events, personality, and health: An inquiry into hardiness, *Journal of Personality and Social Psychology*, 37(1): 1–11.

Koenen, K. C., Driver, K. L., Oscar-Berman, M., Wolfe, J., Folsom, S., Huang, M. T., and Schlesinger, L. (2001) Measures of prefrontal system dysfunction in post-traumatic stress disorder, *Brain and Cognition*, 45(1): 62–78.

Konuk, E., Knipe, J., Eke, I., Yuksek, H., Yurtsever, A., and Ostep, S. (2006) Reprocessing (EMDR) Therapy on Posttraumatic Stress Disorder in Survivors of the 1999 Marmara, Turkey Earthquake, *International Journal of Stress Management*, 13(3): 291–308.

Korte, S. M., Koolhaas, J. M., Wingfield, J. C., and McEwen, B. S. (2005) The Darwinian concept of stress: Benefits of allostasis and costs of allostatic load and the trade-offs in health and disease, *Neuroscience & Biobehavioral Reviews*, 29(1): 3–38.

La Greca, A. M., Silverman, W. K., Vernberg, E. M., and Roberts, M. C. (2002) *Helping Children Cope with Disasters and Terrorism*, Washington, DC: American Psychological Association.

Lambert, K. G. (2003) The life and career of Paul MacLean: A journey towards neurobiological and social harmony, *Physiology and Behavior*, 79(3): 342–340.

Layne, C. M., Pynoos, R. S., Saltzman, W. R., Arslanagic, B., Black, M., Savjak, N., Popovic, T., Durakovic, E., Music, M., Campara, N., Djapo, N., and Hourston, R. (2001) Trauma/grief focused group psychotherapy school-based postwar intervention with traumatized Bosnian adolescents, *Group Dynamics: Theory, Research and Practice*, 5(4): 227–290.

Lazarus, A. (1989) *The Practice of Multimodal Therapy: Systematic, Comprehensive, and Effective Psychotherapy*, Baltimore, MD: Johns Hopkins University Press.

Leahy, T., Pretty, G., and Tenenbaum, G. (2003) Childhood sexual abuse narratives in clinically and nonclinically distressed adult survivors, *Professional Psychology: Research and Practice*, 34(6): 657–655.

LeDoux, J. E. (1996) *The Emotional Brain*, New York: Simon and Shuster.

LeDoux, J. E. (2000) Emotion circuits in the brain, *Annual Review of Neuroscience*, 23: 155–184.

LeDoux, J. E. (2012) Rethinking the emotional brain, *Perspective*, 73(4): 653–676.

LeDoux, J. E. and Phelps, E. A. (1993) Emotional networks in the brain, in M. Lewis, J. M. Haviland-Jones, and L. Feldman-Barrett (2008) *Handbook of Emotions*, New York: Guilford Press. Chapter 10.

Lee, C., Gavriel, H., Drummond, P., Richards, J., and Greenwald, R. (2002) Treatment of PTSD: Stress inoculation training with prolonged exposure compared to EMDR, *Journal of Clinical Psychology*, 58(9): 1071–1089.

Leipold, B. and Greve, W. (2009) Resilience: A conceptual bridge between coping and development, *European Psychologist*, 14(1): 40–50.

Leitch, L. and Miller-Karas, E. (2009) A case for using biologically-based mental health intervention in post-earthquake China: evaluation and training in the trauma resiliency model, *International Journal of Emergency Mental Health*, 11(4): 221–233.

Levy, K. N., Ellison, W. D., Scott, L. N., and Bernecker, S. L. (2010) Attachment style, *Journal of Clinical Psychology*, 67(2): 193–203.

Lewis, C. (1999) Police records of crime, in G. Newman (ed.) *Global Report on Crime and Justice*, New York: Oxford University Press/United Nations, pp. 43–64.

Lieberman, A., Van Horn, P., and Ippen, C. G. (2005) Toward evidence-based treatment: Child–parent psychotherapy with preschoolers exposed to marital violence, *Journal of the American Academy of Child and Adolescent Psychiatry*, 44(12): 1241–1248.

Lieberman, A. F., Ippen, G. C., and Van Horn, P. (2006) Child–parent psychotherapy: 6-month follow-up of a randomized controlled trial, *Journal of the American Academy of Child and Adolescent Psychiatry*, 45(8): 913–918.

Lieberman, A., Van Horn, P., Grandison, C., and Pekarsky, J. (1997) Mental health assessment of infants, toddlers, and preschoolers in a service program and a treatment outcome research program, *Infant Mental Health Journal*, 18(2): 158–170.

Lindström, B. and Eriksson, M. (2006) Contextualizing salutogenesis and Antonovsky in public health development, *Health Promotion International*, 21(3): 238–244.

Linehan, M. M. (1993) *Cognitive Behavioral Treatment of Borderline Personality Disorder*, New York: Guilford Press.

Linehan, M. M., Armstrong, H. E., Suarez, A., Allmon, D., and Heard, H. (1991) Cognitive-Behavioral treatment of chronically parasuicidal borderline patients, *Archives of General Psychiatry*, 48(12): 1060–1064.

Linnman, C. Zeidan, M. A., Furtak, S. C., Pitman, R. K., Quirk, G. J., and Milad, M. R. (2012) Resting amygdala and medial prefrontal metabolisms predict functional activation of the fear extinction circuit, *American Journal of Psychiatry*, 169(4): 415–419.

Liston, C., McEwen, B. S., and Casey, B. J. (2009) Psychosocial stress reversibly disrupts prefrontal processing and attentional control, *Proceedings of the National Academy of Sciences of the United States of America*, 106(3): 912–917.

Littleton, H., Grill-Taquechel, A., and Axsom, D. (2009) Impaired and incapacitated rape victims: Assault characteristics and post-assault experiences, *Violence and Victims*, 24(4): 439–459.

Litz, B. T. and Gray, M. J. (2002) Early intervention for mass violence: What is the evidence? What should be done? *Cognitive and Behavioral Practice*, 9(4): 266–272.

Luecken, L. J., Appelhans, B. M., Kraft, A., and Brown, A. (2006) Never far from home: A cognitive-affective model of the impact of early-life family relationships on physiological stress responses in adulthood, *Journal of Social and Personal Relationships*, 23(2): 189–203.

Luther, S. S., Cicchetti, D., and Becker, B. (2000) The construct of resilience: A critical evaluation and guidelines for future work, *Child Development*, 71(3): 543–562, available at: www.ncbi.nlm.nih.gov/pmc/articles/PMC1885202/pdf/nihms-21559.pdf.

Lydiard, R. B. and Hamner, M. (2009) Clinical importance of sleep disturbance as a treatment target in PTSD, *FOCUS The Journal of Lifelong Learning in Psychiatry*, 7(2): 176–183.

McCann, L. I. and Pearlman, L. A. (1990) Vicarious traumatization: A framework for understanding the psychological effects of working with victims, *Journal of Traumatic Stress*, 3(1): 131–149.

McEwen, B. S. (2008) Understanding the potency of stressful early life experiences on brain and body function, *Metabolism*, 57(Supp. 2): S11–S15.

McEwen, B. S. (2013) Hormones and the social brain, *Science*, 339(6117): 279–280.

McEwen, B. S., Eiland, L., Hunter, R. G., and Miller, M. M. (2012) Stress and anxiety: structural plasticity and epigenetic regulation as a consequence of stress, *Neuropharmacology*, 62(1): 3–12.

McGaugh, J. L. and Roozendaal, B. (2002) Role of adrenal stress hormones in forming lasting memories in the brain, *Current Opinion in Neurobiology*, 12(2): 205–210.

McHugo, G. J., Kammerer, N., Jackson, E. W., Markoff, L. S., Gatz, M. Larson, M. J., Mazelis, R., and Hennigan, K. (2005) Women, co-occurring disorders, and violence study: Evaluation design and study population, *Journal of Substance Abuse Treatment*, 28(2): 91–107.

McLay, R., Graap, K., Spira, J., Perlman, K., Johnston, S., Rothbaum, B., Difede, J., Deal, W., Oliver, D., Baird, A., Bordnick, P., Spitalnick, J., Pyne, J., and Rizzo, A. (2012) Development and testing of virtual reality exposure therapy for post-traumatic stress disorder in active duty service members who served in Iraq and Afghanistan, *Military Medicine*, 177(6): 635–642.

McLean, C. and Foa, E. (2011) Prolonged exposure therapy for post-traumatic stress disorder: a review of the evidence and dissemination, *Expert Review*, 11(8): 1151–1163.

McNally, R. J. (2007) Mechanisms of exposure therapy: how neuroscience can improve psychological treatments for anxiety disorders, *Clinical Psychology Review*, 27(6): 750–759.

McNally, R. J., Bryant, R. A., and Ehlers, A. (2003) Does early psychological intervention promote recovery from posttraumatic stress? *Psychological Science in the Public Interest*, 4(2): 45–79.

McSherry, W. C. and Holm, J. (1994) Sense of coherence: its effects on psychological and physiological processes prior to, during, and after a stressful situation, *Journal of Clinical Psychology*, 50(4): 476–487.

Madrid, P. A. and Grant, R. (2008) Meeting mental health needs following a natural disaster: Lessons from Hurricane Katrina, *Professional Psychology: Research and Practice*, 39(1): 86–92.

Maheu, F. S., Dozier, M., Guyer, A. E., Mandell, D., Peloso, E., Poeth, K., Jenness, J., Lau, J. Y. F., Ackerman, J. P., Pine, D. S., and Ernst, M. (2010) A preliminary study of medial temporal lobe function in youths with a history of caregiver deprivation and emotional neglect, *Cognitive, Affective, & Behavioral Neuroscience*, 10(1): 34–49.

Mak, W., Ng, I., and Wong, C. (2011) Resilience: Enhancing well-being through the positive cognitive triad, *Journal of Counseling Psychology*, 58(4): 610–617.

Makinson, R. and Young, J. S. (2012) Cognitive behavioral therapy and the treatment of posttraumatic stress disorder: Where counseling and neuroscience meet, *Journal of Counseling and Development*, 90(2): 131–140.

Malchiodi, C. (2011) Trauma informed art therapy with sexually abused children, in P. Goodyear-Brown (ed.) *Handbook of Child Sexual Abuse: Prevention, Assessment, and Treatment*, New York: Wiley, Chapter 15.

Marmar, C. (2009) Mental health impact of Afghanistan and Iraq deployment: Meeting the challenge of a new generation of veterans, *Depression and Anxiety*, 26(6): 493–497.

Mashiach, R., Freedman, S., Bargai, N., Boker, R., Hadar, H. and Shalev, A. (2004) Coping with trauma: Narrative and cognitive perspectives, *Psychiatry*, 67(3): 280–293.

Masten, A. (2001) Ordinary magic: Resilience processes in development, *American Psychologist*, 56(3): 227–238.

Matto, H. C. and Strolin-Goltzman, G. J. (2010) Integrating social neuroscience and social work: Innovations for advancing practice-based research, *Social Work*, 55(2): 147–156.

Maxfield, L. (2009) Twenty years of EMDR, *Journal of EMDR Practice and Research*, 3(3): 4–5.

Mead, H., Beauchaine, T., and Shannon, K. (2010) Neurobiological adaptations to violence across development, *Development and Psychopathology*, 22(1): 1–22.

Meekums, B. (1999) A creative model for recovery from child sexual abuse trauma, *The Arts in Psychotherapy*, 26(4): 247–259.

Meichenbaum, D. (2007) Stress inoculation training: A preventative and treatment approach, in P. Lehrer, R. Woolfolk, and W. Sime (eds.) *Principles and Practice of Stress Management*, 3rd edition, New York: Guilford Press.

Mendes, D. D., Feijó Mello, M., Ventura, P. de Medeiros Passarela, C., and de Jesus Mari, J. (2008) A systematic review of the effectiveness of cognitive behavioral therapy for posttraumatic stress disorder, *International Journal of Psychiatry in Medicine*, 38(3): 241–259.

Micale, M. L. (ed.) (2001) *Traumatic Pasts: History, Psychiatry, and Trauma in Modern Age, 1870–1930*, Cambridge: Cambridge University Press.

Miller, L. (1998) Psychotherapy of crime victims: Treating the aftermath of interpersonal violence, *Psychotherapy*, 35(3): 336–345.

Miller, T. W. (2007) Trauma, change, and psychological health in the 21st century, *American Psychologist*, 62(8): 889–898.

Mills, M. A., Edmondson, M. A., and Park, C. L. (2007) Trauma and stress response among Hurricane Katrina evacuees, *American Journal of Public Health*, 97(1): 116–123.

Monson, C., Schnurr, P., Resick, P., Friedman, M., Young-Xu, Y., and Stevens, S. (2006) Cognitive processing therapy for veterans with military-related posttraumatic stress disorder, *Journal of Consulting and Clinical Psychology*, 74(5): 898–907.

Montpetit, M. A., Bergeman, C. S., Deboeck, P. R., Tiberio, S. S., and Boker, S. M. (2010) Resilience-as-process: Negative affect, stress, and coupled dynamical systems, *Psychology and Aging*, 25(3): 631–640.

Morrison, I. and Clift, S. (2006) Mental health promotion through supported further education: The value of Antonovsky's salutogenic model of health, *Health Education*, 106(5): 365–380.

Muller, R., Sicoli, L., and Lemieux, K. (2000) Relationship between attachment style and posttraumatic stress symptomatology among adults who report the experience of childhood abuse, *Journal of Traumatic Stress*, 13(2): 321–332.

Najavits, L. M. (2009) Seeking Safety: An implementation guide, in A. Rubin and D. W. Springer (eds.) *A Clinician's Guide to Evidence-Based Practice*, Hoboken, NJ: John Wiley.

National Center for PTSD (2007) *Treatment of PTSD*, Washington, DC: United States Department of Veterans Affairs, available at: www.ptsd.va.gov/public/pages/treatment-ptsd.asp.

National Center on Domestic Violence, Trauma, and Mental Health. (2012) Creating Trauma-Informed Services Tipsheet Series, available at: www.nationalcenterdvtraumamh.org/publications-products/creating-trauma-informed-services-tipsheet-series-for-advocates/.

National Institute for Clinical Excellence (2005) *Post-Traumatic Stress Disorder (PTSD): The Management of PTSD in Adults and Children in Primary and Secondary Care*, Clinical Guideline 26, London: National Collaborating Centre for Mental Health.

NATO (2011) Financial and economic data relating to NATO Defense, North Atlantic Treaty Organization, available at: www.nato.int/nato_static/assets/pdf/pdf_2011_03/20110309_PR_CP_2011_027.pdf.

NCTIC (National Center for Trauma-Informed Care) (n.d.) Website, available at: www.samhsa.gov/nctic/trauma.asp.

NCTSN (National Child Traumatic Stress Network) (n.d.) *Trauma-Focused Cognitive Behavioral Therapy (TF-CBT)*, available at: www.nctsn.org/nctsn_assets/pdfs/promising_practices/TF-CBT_fact_sheet_3-20-07.pdf (accessed June 3, 2013).

Neria, Y. B. (2010) A longitudinal study of Post-Traumatic Stress Disorder, depression, and generalized anxiety disorder in Israeli civilians exposed to war trauma, *Journal of Traumatic Stress*, 23(3): 322–330.

Neville, K. and Cole, D. A. (2013) The relationship among health promotion behaviors, compassion fatigue, burnout, and compassion satisfaction in nurses practicing in a community medical center, *JONA: The Journal of Nursing Administration*, 43(6): 348–354.

Nichols, M. (2013) *Family Therapy Concepts and Methods*, 10th edition, Boston, MA: Pearson.

Nickerson, A., Aderka, I. M., Bryant, R. A., and Hofmann, S. G. (2012) The relationship between childhood exposure to trauma and intermittent explosive disorder, *Psychiatry Research*, 197(1/2): 128–134.

Norman, S., Wilkins, K., Tapert, S., Lang, A., and Najavits, L. (2010) A pilot study of Seeking Safety therapy with OEF/OIF Veterans, *Journal of Psychoactive Drug*, 42(1): 83–87.

NREPP (National Registry of Evidence-based Programs and Practice) (n.d.) Website, available at: www.nrepp.samhsa.gov.

Ong, A. D., Bergeman, C. S., Bisconti, T. L., and Wallace, K. A. (2006) Psychological resilience, positive emotions, and successful adaptation to stress in later life, *Journal of Personality and Social Psychology*, 91(4): 730–749.

Opris, D., Pintea, S., Garcia-Palacios, A., Botella, C., Szamoskozi, S., and David, D. (2012) Virtual Reality Exposure Therapy in anxiety disorders: A quantitative meta-analysis, *Depression and Anxiety*, 29(2): 85–93.

O'Toole, B. I., Catts, S. V., Outram, S. Pierse, K. R., and Cockburn, J. (2009) The physical and mental health of Australian Vietnam veterans 3 decades after the war and its relation to military service, combat, and posttraumatic stress disorder, *American Journal of Epidemiology*, 170(3): 318–330.

Pechtel, P. and Pizzagalli, D. A. (2011) Effects of early life stress on cognitive and affective function: an integrated review of human literature, *Psychopharmacology*, 214(1): 55–70.

Peres, J. F. P., McFarlane, A., Nasello, A. G., and Moores, K. A. (2008) Traumatic memories: Bridging the gap between functional neuroimaging and psychotherapy, *Australian and New Zealand Journal of Psychiatry*, 42(6): 478–488.

Perry, B. D. (2001) The neurodevelopmental impact of violence in childhood, in D. Schetky and E. P. Benedek (eds.) *Textbook of Child and Adolescent Forensic Psychiatry*, Washington, DC: American Psychiatric Press, Inc.

Perry, B. D (2006) Fear and learning: Trauma-related factors in the adult education process, *New Directions for Adult and Continuing Education*, 2006(110): 21–27.

Perry, B. D. (2009) Examining child maltreatment through a neurodevelopmental lens: Clinical applications of the Neurosequential Model of Therapeutics, *Journal of Loss and Trauma*, 14(4): 240–255.

Perry, B. D. and Hambrick, E. P. (2008) The Neurosequential Model of Therapeutics, *Reclaiming Children and Youth*, 17(3): 38–43.

Pierrehumbert, B., Torrisi, R., Laufer, D., and Halfon, O. (2010) Oxytocin response to an experimental psychosocial challenge in adults exposed to traumatic experiences during childhood or adolescence, *Neuroscience*, 166(1): 168–177.

Pierrehumbert, B., Torrisi, R., Ansermet, F., Borghini, A., and Halfon, O. (2012) Adult attachment representations predict cortisol and oxytocin responses to stress, *Attachment & Human Development*, 14(5): 453–476.

Pine, D. S. and Cohen, J. A. (2002) Trauma in children and adolescents: risk and treatment of psychiatric sequelae, *Biological Psychiatry*, 51(7): 519–531.

Pine, D. S., Costello, J., and Masten, A. (2005) Trauma, proximity, and developmental psychopathology: the effects of war and terrorism on children, *Neuropsychopharmacology*, 30(10): 1781–1782.

Pinheiro, P. S. (2006) *World Report on Violence Against Children*, Geneva: United Nations, available at: www.unicef.org/lac/full_tex%283%29.pdf.

Plummer, J. and Knudson-Martin, C. (1996) Narrative of escape: a hermeneutic study of resiliency, *Contemporary Family Therapy*, 18(4): 567–587.

Prot, K. (2010) Late effects of trauma: PTSD in holocaust survivors, *Journal of Loss and Trauma*, 15(1): 28–42.

Radan, A. (2007) Exposure to violence and expressions of resilience in Central American women survivors of war, *Journal of Aggression, Maltreatment and Trauma*, 14(1): 147–164.

Radey, M. and Figley, C. (2007) The social psychology of compassion, *Clinical Social Work Journal*, 35(3): 207–214.

Ramchandani, P. and Jones, D. (2003) Treating psychological symptoms in sexually abused children, *British Journal of Psychiatry*, 183(6): 484–490.

Rao, U., Chen, L., Bidesi, A. S., Shad, M. U., Thomas, M. A., and Hammen, C. L. (2010) Hippocampal changes associated with early-life adversity and vulnerability to depression, *Biological Psychiatry*, 67(4): 357–364.

Rauch, S. L., van der Kolk, B. A., Fisler, R. E., Alpert, N. M., Orr, S. P., Savage, C. R., Fischman, A. J., Jenike, M. A., and Pitman, R. K. (1996) A symptom provocation study of posttraumatic stress disorder using positron emission tomography and script-driven imagery, *Archives of General Psychiatry*, 53(5): 380–387.

Reger, G. M., Holloway, K. M., Candy, C., Rothbaum, B., Difede, J., Rizzo, A., and Gahm, G. (2011) Effectiveness of virtual reality exposure therapy for active duty soldiers in a military mental health clinic, *Journal of Traumatic Stress*, 24(1): 93–96.

Rennison, C. M. (2002) *Rape and Sexual Assault: Reporting to the Police and Medical Attention, 1992–2000*, US Department of Justice, Bureau of Justice Statistics, available at: www.bjs.gov/content/pub/ascii/rsarp00.txt.

Resick, P. A. and Schnicke, M. K. (1992) Cognitive processing therapy for sexual assault victims, *Journal of Consulting and Clinical Psychology*, 60(5): 748–756.

Resick, P. A., Nishith, P., Weaver, T., Astin, M., and Feuer, C. (2002) A comparison of Cognitive-Processing Therapy with prolonged exposure and a waiting condition for the treatment of chronic posttraumatic stress disorder in female rape victims, *Journal of Consulting and Clinical Psychology*, 70(4): 867–879.

Resick, P. A., Williams, L., Suvak, M., Monson, C., and Gradus, J. (2012) Long-term outcomes of cognitive-behavioral treatments for posttraumatic stress disorder among female rape survivors, *Journal of Consulting and Clinical Psychology*, 80(2): 201–210.

Reyes, C. and Asbrand, J. (2005) A longitudinal study assessing trauma symptoms in sexually abused children engaged in play therapy, *International Journal of Play Therapy*, 14(2): 25–47.

Rizzo, A., Parsons, T. D., Lange, B., Kenny, P., Buckwalter, J. G., Rothbaum, B., Difede, J., Frazier, J., Newman, B., Williams, J., and Reger, G. (2011) Virtual reality goes to war: a brief review of the future of military behavioral healthcare, *Journal of Clinical Psychology Medical Settings*, 18(2): 176–187.

Roche, D., Runtz, M., and Hunter, M. (1999) Adult attachment: a mediator between child sexual abuse and later psychological adjustment, *Journal of Interpersonal Violence*, 14(184): 151–163.

Rodin, D. and van Ommeren, M. (2009) Commentary: Explaining enormous variations of rates of disorder in trauma-focused psychiatric epidemiology after major emergencies, *International Journal of Epidemiology*, 38(4): 1045–1048.

Rodrigues, S., LeDoux, J., and Sapolsky, R. (2009) The influence of stress hormones on fear circuitry, *Annual Review of Neuroscience*, 32: 289–313.

Rogan, M. T., Stäubli, U. V., and LeDoux, J. E. (1997) Fear conditioning induces associative long-term potentiation of the amygdala, *Nature*, 390: 604–607, available at: www.nature.com/nature/journal/v390/n6660/full/390604a0.html.

Rose, S., Bisson, J., and Wessely, S. (2003) A systematic review of single-session psychological interventions ("debriefing") following trauma, *Psychotherapy and Psychosomatics*, 72(4): 176–184.

Rose, S., Freeman, C., and Proudlock, S. (2012) Despite the evidence – why are we still not creating more trauma informed mental health services? *Journal of Public Mental Health*, 11(1): 5–9.

Rothbaum, B. O., Hodges, L., Alarcon, R., Ready, D., Shahar, F., Graap, K., Pair, J., Hebert, P., Gotz, D., Wills, B., and Baltzell, D. (1999) Virtual reality exposure therapy for PTSD Vietnam veterans: A case study, *Journal of Traumatic Stress*, 12(2): 263–271.

Rudy, J. W., Huff, N. C., and Matus-Amat, P. (2004) Understanding contextual fear conditioning: Insights from a two-process model, *Neuroscience and Biobehavioral Reviews*, 28(7): 675–685.

Russell, M., Silver, S., Rogers, S., and Darnell, J. (2007) Responding to an identified need: A joint Department of Defense/Department of Veterans Affairs training program in eye movement desensitization and reprocessing (EMDR) for clinicians providing trauma services, *International Journal of Stress Management*, 14(6): 1–71.

Ruzek, L. I., Curran, E., Friedman, M. J., Gusman, F. D., Southwick, S. M., Swales, P., Walser, R. D., Watson, P. J., and Whealin, J. (2007) Treatment of the returning Iraq war veteran, *National Center for PTSD*, available at: www.ptsd.va.gov/professional/pages/treatment-iraq-vets.asp.

Ryan, B., Bashant, C., and Brooks, D. (2006) Protecting and supporting children in the child welfare system and the juvenile court, *Juvenile and Family Court Journal*, 57(1): 61–69.

Sadock, B. and Sadock, V. (2007) *Kaplan and Sadock's Synopsis of Psychiatry*, 10th edition, Philadelphia, PA: Lippencott Wilkins and Williams.

Salvatore, R. (2009) Posttraumatic Stress Disorder: A treatable public health problem, *Health and Social Work*, 34(2): 153–155.

Sansone, R. A., Whitecar, P., and Wiederman, M. W. (2009) The prevalence of childhood trauma among those seeking buprenorphine treatment, *Journal of Addictive Diseases*, 28(1): 64–67.

Sapolsky, R. M. (2003) Stress and plasticity in the limbic system, *Neurochemical Research*, 28(11): 1735–1742.

Sapolsky, R. M. (2004) *Why Zebras Don't Get Ulcers*, 3rd edition, New York: Henry Holt Publishers.

Sapolsky, R. M., Romero, L. M., and Munck, A. U. (2000) How do glucocorticoids influence stress responses: Integrating permissive, suppressive, stimulatory, and preparative actions, *Endocrine Reviews*, 21(1): 55–89.

Sardu, C., Mereu, A., Sotgiu, A., Andrissi, L., Jacobson, M. K., and Contu, P. (2012) Antonovsky's Sense of Coherence Scale: Cultural validation of SOC questionnaire and socio-demographic patterns in an Italian population, *Clinical Practice and Epidemiology in Mental Health*, 8: 1–6, available at: www.ncbi.nlm.nih.gov/pmc/articles/PMC3282882/.

Schechter, D. S., Moser, D. A., McCaw, J. E., and Myers, M. M. (2013) Autonomic functioning in mothers with interpersonal violence–related posttraumatic stress disorder in response to separation–reunion, *Developmental Psychobiology*, pp. 1–13, DOI: 10.1002/dev.21144 (ahead of print).

Scheeringa, M. S., Salloum, A., Arnberger, R. A., Weems, C. F., Amaya-Jackson, L., and Cohen, J. A. (2007) Feasibility and effectiveness of cognitive–behavioral therapy for posttraumatic stress disorder in preschool children: Two case reports, *Journal of Traumatic Stress*, 20(4): 631–636.

Scheier, M. F. and Carver, C. S. (1985) Optimism, coping, and health: Assessment and implications of generalized outcome expectancies, *Health Psychology*, 4(3): 219–247.

Schmahl, C., Berne, K., Krause, A., Kleindienst, N., Valerius, G., Vermetten, E., and Bohus, M. (2009) Hippocampus and amygdala volumes in patients with borderline personality disorder with or without posttraumatic stress disorder, *Journal of Psychiatry and Neuroscience*, 34(4): 289–295.

Schnurr, P. and Friedman, M. (2008) Treatments for PTSD: Understanding the evidence, *PTSD Research Quarterly*, 19(3): 1050–1835, available at: www.ptsd.va.gov/professional/newsletters/research-quarterly/V19N3.pdf.

Schnurr, P., Friedman, M., Engel, C., Foa, E., Shea, M. T., Chow, B., Resick, P., Thurston, V., Orsillo, S., Haug, R., Turner, C., and Bernardy, N. (2007) Cognitive behavioral therapy for posttraumatic stress disorder in women: A randomized control trial, *Journal of the American Medical Association*, 297(8): 820–830.

Schumacher, J., Coffey, S., Norris, F., Tracy, M., Clements, K., and Galea, S. (2010) Intimate partner violence and Hurricane Katrina: Predictors and associated mental health outcomes, *Violence and Victims*, 25(5): 588–603.

Sehlmeyer, C., Dannlowski, U., Schöning, S., Kugel, H. Pyka, M., Pfleiderer, B., Zwitserlood, P., Schiffbauer, H., Heindel, W., Arolt, V., and Konrad, C. (2011) Neural correlates of trait anxiety in fear extinction, *Psychological Medicine*, 41(4): 789–798.

Shakespeare-Finch, J. and Armstrong, D. (2010) Trauma type and posttrauma outcomes: differences between survivors of motor vehicle accidents, sexual assault, and bereavement, *Journal of Loss and Trauma*, 15(2): 69–82.

Shapiro, F. (2007) EMDR, Adaptive information processing and case conceptualization, *Journal of EMDR Practice and Research*, 1(2): 68–87.

Shapiro, F. and Laliotis, D. (2011) EMDR and the Adaptive Information Processing Model: Integrative treatment and case conceptualization, *Journal of Clinical Social Work*, 39(2): 191–200.

Sharan, P. L. (2007) *Research Capacity for Mental Health in Low-and-Middle-Income Countries: Results of a Mapping Project*, available at: www.who.int/mental_health/MHRC_FullText.pdf.

Sharpless, B. A. and Barber, J. P. (2011) A clinician's guide to PTSD treatments for returning veterans, *Professional Psychology: Research and Practice*, 42(1): 8–15.

Sheikh, A. L. (2008) Theory and practice, *Counseling Psychology Quarterly*, 21(1): 85–97.

Shuster, M. A., Stein, B. D., Jaycox, L. H., Collins, R. L., Marshall, G. N., Elliott, M. N., Zhou, A. J., Kanouse, D. E., Morrison, J. L., and Berry, S. H. (2001) A national survey of stress reactions after the September 11, 2001 terrorist attacks, *New England Journal of Medicine*, 345(20): 1507–1512.

Silove, D., Momartin, S., Marnan, C., Steel, Z., and Manicavasagar, V. (2010) Adult separation anxiety disorder among war-affected Bosnian refugees: Comorbidity with PTSD and associations with dimensions of trauma, *Journal of Traumatic Stress*, 23(1): 169–172.

Silva, R., Cloitre, M., Davis, L., Levitt, J., Gomez, S., Ngai, I., and Brown, E. (2003) Early intervention with traumatized children, *Psychiatric Quarterly*, 74(4): 333–347.

Silver, S., Rogers, S., and Russell, M. (2008) Eye Movement Desensitization and Reprocessing (EMDR) in the treatment of war veterans, *Journal of Clinical Psychology: In Session*, 68(8): 947–957.

Snyder, C. R. (2002) Hope theory: Rainbows in the mind, *Psychological Inquiry*, 13(3): 249–275.

Snyder, C. R., Irving, L., and Anderson, J. R. (1991) Hope and health: Measuring the will and the ways, in C. R. Snyder and D. R. Forsyth (eds.) *Handbook of Social and Clinical Psychology: The Health Perspective*, Elmsford, NY: Pergamon.

Somer, E., Ruvio, A., Sever, I., and Soref, E. (2007) Reactions to repeated unpredictable terror attacks: Relationships among exposure, posttraumatic distress, mood, and intensity of coping, *Journal of Applied Social Psychology*, 37(4): 862–886.

Sotres-Bayon, F. (2008) Neural correlates of individual variability of fear extinction, *Journal of Neuroscience*, 28(47): 12147–12149.

Sotres-Bayon, F., Bush, D. E. A., and LeDoux, J. E. (2004) Emotional perseveration: An update on prefrontal-amygdala interactions in fear extinction, *Learning and Memory*, 11(5): 525–535.

Sotres-Bayon, F., Cain, C. K., and LeDoux, J. E. (2006) Brain mechanisms of fear extinction: Historical perspectives of the prefrontal cortex, *Biological Psychiatry*, 60(4): 329–336.

Sowell, E. R., Thompson, P. M., Holmes, C. J., Jernigan, T. L., and Toga, A. W. (1999) In vivo evidence for post-adolescent brain maturation in frontal and striatal regions, *Neuroscience Nature*, 2(10): 859–861, available at: www.loni.ucla.edu/~esowell/nn1099_859.pdf (accessed May 28, 2013).

Stalker, C., Gebotys, R., and Harper, K. (2005) Insecure attachment as a predictor of outcome following inpatient trauma treatment for women survivors of childhood abuse, *Bulletin of the Menninger Clinic*, 69(2): 137–156.

Stauffer, S. (2009) Trauma and disorganized attachment in refugee children: Integrating theories and exploring treatment options, *UNHCR Refugee Survey Quarterly*, 27(4): 150–163.

Steel, Z. S. (2009) Human rights and the trauma model: Genuine partners or uneasy allies? *Journal of Traumatic Stress*, 22(5): 358–365.

Steil, R., Dyer, A., Priebe, K., Kleindienst, N., and Bohus, M. (2011) Dialectical Behavior Therapy for posttraumatic stress disorder related to childhood sexual abuse: a pilot study of an intensive residential treatment program, *Journal of Traumatic Stress*, 24(1): 102–106.

Stephenson, R., Jadhav, A., and Hindin, M. (2013) Physical domestic violence and subsequent contraceptive adoption among women in rural India, *Journal of Interpersonal Violence*, 28(5): 1020–1039.

Swales, M., Heard, H. L., Williams, J., and Mark, G. (2000) Linehan's dialectical behavior therapy (DBT) for borderline personality disorder: Overview and adaptation, *Journal of Mental Health*, 9(1): 7–23.

Sweezy, M. (2011) Treating trauma after dialectical behavioral therapy, *Journal of Psychotherapy Integration*, 21(1): 90–102.

Tamminga, C. A. (2006) The anatomy of fear extinction, *The American Journal of Psychiatry*, 163(6): 961.

Tarquinio, C., Schmitt, A., Tarquinio, P., Rydberg, A.-A., and Spitz, E. (2012) Benefits of "eye movement desensitization and reprocessing" psychotherapy in the treatment of female victims of intimate partner rape, *Sexologies*, 21(2): 60–67.

Taylor, S. E., Klein, L. C., Lewis, B. P., Gruenewald, T. L., Gurung, R. A. R., and Updegraff, J. A. (2000) Biobehavioral responses to stress in females: Tend-and-befriend, not fight-or-flight, *Psychological Review*, 107(3): 411–429.

Tedeschi, R. G. and Calhoun, L. G. (2004) Posttraumatic growth: Conceptual foundations and empirical evidence, *Psychological Inquiry*, 15(1): 1–18.

Tedeschi, R. G. and Kilmer, R. P. (2005) Assessing strengths, resilience, and growth to guide clinical interventions, *Professional Psychology: Research and Practice*, 36(3): 230–237.

Tehrani, N. (2009) Compassion fatigue: experiences in occupational health, human resources, counselling and police, *Occupational Medicine*, 60: 133–138.

Thienkrua, W., Cardozo, B. L., Chakkraband, M. L. S., Guadamuz, T. E., Pengjuntr, W., Tantipiwatanaskul, P., Sakornsatian, S., Ekassawin, S., Panyayong, B., Varangrat, A., Tappero, J. W., Schreiber, M., and Van Griensven, F. (2006) Symptoms of posttraumatic stress disorder and depression among children in tsunami-affected areas in southern Thailand, *JAMA: The Journal Of The American Medical Association*, 296(5): 549–559.

Thomas, J. (2013) Association of personal distress with burnout, compassion fatigue, and compassion satisfaction among clinical social workers, *Journal of Social Service Research*, 39(3): 365–379.

Tosone, C., McTighe, J. P., Bauwens, J., and Naturale, A. (2011) Shared traumatic stress and the long-term impact of 9/11 on Manhattan clinicians, *Journal of Traumatic Stress*, 24(5): 546–552.

Tuerk, P., Grubaugh, A., Hamner, M., and Foa, E. (2009) Diagnosis and treatment of PTSD related compulsive checking behaviors in veterans of the Iraq war: The influence of military context on the expression of PTSD Symptoms, *American Journal of Psychiatry*, 166(7): 762–767.

Tuerk, P. W., Wangelin, B., Rauch, S. A. M., Dismuke, C. E., Yoder, M., Myrick, H., Eftekhari, A., and Acierno, R. (2012) Health service utilization before and after evidence-based treatment for PTSD, *Psychological Services*, advanced online publication. DOI: 10.1037/a0030549.

Twardosz, S. and Lutzker, J. R. (2010) Child maltreatment and the developing brain: A review of neuroscience perspectives, *Aggression and Violent Behavior*, 15(1): 59–68.

Tworus, R., Szymanska, S., and IInicki, S. (2010) A soldier suffering from PTSD treated by controlled stress exposition using virtual reality and behavioral training, *Cyberpsychology, Behavior, and Social Networking*, 13(1): 103–107.

UNHCR (2011) *Statistical Yearbook 2011*, available from: www.unhcr.org/516282cf5.html.

UNISDR (2012) *Annual Report 2012 prepared for United Nations Office for Disaster Risk Reduction*, available from: www.unisdr.org/we/inform/publications/33363.

US Census Bureau (2012) National security and veterans affairs: Veterans, *The 2012 Statistical Abstract: The National Data Book*, available at: www.census.gov/compendia/statab/cats/national_security_veterans_affairs/veterans.html.

US Department of Health and Human Services (n.d.) Treatment and trauma-informed care, Available at: https://www.childwelfare.gov/responding/trauma.cfm.

US Department of Veterans Affairs (2012) Veterans posttraumatic stress disorder (PTSD), *Office of Public and Intergovernmental Affairs*, available at: www.va.gov/opa/issues/ptsd.asp.

Uvnäs Moberg, K. (1997) Physiological and endocrine effects of social contact, *Annals of the New York Academy of Sciences*, 807(1): 146–163.

Uvnäs Moberg, K. (2003) *The Oxytocin Factor: Tapping the Hormone of Calm, Love, and Healing*, Cambridge, MA: Da Capo Press.

van der Kolk, B. A. (2002) Posttraumatic therapy in the age of neuroscience, *Psychoanalytic Dialogues*, 12(3): 381–392.

van der Kolk, B. A. (2006) Clinical implications of neuroscience research in PTSD, *Annals New York Academy of Sciences*, 1071: 277–293.

van der Kolk, B. A., Roth, S., Pelcovitz, D., Sunday, S., and Spinazolla, J. (2005) Disorders of extreme stress: The empirical foundation of complex adaptation to trauma, *Journal of Traumatic Stress*, 10(5): 389–399.

Van Fleet, R., Lilly, J., and Kaduson, H. (1999) Play therapy for children exposed to violence: Individual, family and community interventions, *International Journal of Play Therapy*, 8(1): 27–42.

Van Vliet, K. J. (2008) Shame and resilience in adulthood: A grounded theory study, *Journal of Counseling Psychology*, 55(2): 233–245.

Vázquez, C., Cervellón, P., Pérez-Sales, P., Vidales, D., and Gaborit, M. (2005) Positive emotions in earthquake survivors in El Salvador, *Journal of Anxiety Disorders*, 17(3): 313–328.

Versola-Russo, J. (2006) Workplace violence: Vicarious trauma in the psychiatric setting, *Journal of Police Crisis Negotiations*, 6(2): 79–103.

Vickerman, K. A., and Margolin, G. (2007) Posttraumatic stress in children and adolescents exposed to family violence: II. Treatment, *Professional Psychology: Research and Practice*, 38(6): 620–628.

Vieth, H. (2009) Mental health policies in Europe, *Euro Observer*, 11(3): 1–15.

Vos, F., Rodriguez, J., Below, R., and Guha-Sapir, D. (2010) *Annual Disasters Statistical Review 2009: The numbers and trends*, available at: www.cred.be/sites/default/files/ADSR_2009.pdf (accessed February 8, 2013).

Walsh, K., Blaustein, M., Knight, W. G., Spinazzola, J., and van der Kolk, B. A. (2007) Resiliency factors in the relation between childhood sexual abuse and adulthood sexual assault in college-age women, *Journal of Child Sexual Abuse*, 16(1): 1–17.

Weiner, D., Schneider, A., and Lyons, J. (2009) Evidence-based treatments for trauma among culturally diverse foster care youth: Treatment retentions and outcomes, *Children and Youth Services Review*, 31(11): 1199–1205.

Weiss, D. S. and Marmar, C. R. (1997) The Impact of Event Scale – revised, in J. P. Wilson and T. M. Keane (eds.) *Assessing Psychological Trauma and PTSD*, New York: Guilford Press, pp. 399–411.

Westphal, M., Bonanno, G. A., and Bartone, P. (2008) Resilience and personality, in B. Lukey and V. Tepe,(eds.) *Biobehavioral Resilience to Stress*, New York: Taylor and Francis.

White, M. (2003) Narrative practice and community assignments, *International Journal of Narrative Therapy and Community Work*, 3(2): 17–56.

White, M. and Epston, D. (1990) *Narrative Means to Therapeutic Ends*, New York: Norton.

Wong, D. F. K. (2008) Differential impacts of stressful life events and social support on the mental health of mainland Chinese immigrant and local youth in Hong Kong: A resilience perspective, *British Journal of Social Work*, 38(2): 236–252.

World Health Organization (2001) *World Health Report 2001*, available from: www.who.int/whr/2001/en/whr01_en.pdf.

World Health Organization (2005) *Promoting Mental Health: Concepts, Emerging Evidence, Practice*, H. S. Herrman (ed.), Geneva, Switzerland: World Health Organization, available at: www.who.int/mental_health/evidence/MH_Promotion_Book.pdf.

Yehuda, R. (2002) Current status of cortisol findings in post-traumatic stress disorder, *Psychiatric Clinics of North America*, 25(2): 341–368.

Yehuda, R. (2006) Advances in understanding neuroendocrine alterations in PTSD, and their therapeutic implications, *Annals of the New York Academy of Science*, 1071: 137–166.

Yehuda, R. and LeDoux, J. (2007) Response variation following trauma: A translational neuroscience approach to understanding PTSD, *Neuron*, 56(1): 19–32.

Zang, Y., Hunt, N., and Cox, T. (2013) A randomized controlled pilot study: the effectiveness of narrative exposure therapy with adult survivors of the Sichuan earthquake, *BMC Psychiatry*, 13(41): 1–11.

Zappert, L. and Westrup, D. (2008) Cognitive Processing Therapy for posttraumatic stress disorder in residential setting, *Psychotherapy Theory, Research, Practice, Training*, 45(3): 361–376.

Zoladz, P. R. and Diamond, D. M. (2013) Current status on behavioral and biological markers of PTSD: A search for clarity in a conflicting literature, *Neuroscience and Biobehavioral Science Reviews*, 37(5): 860–895.

Zuatra, A., Smith, B., Affleck, G., and Tennen, H. (2001) Examinations of chronic pain and affect relationships: applications of a Dynamic Model of Affect, *Journal of Consulting and Clinical Psychology*, 69(5): 786–795.

Index

Locators in **bold** refer to figures/diagrams